Self-Worth Without Self-Worship:

The Bible-Based Approach to Self-Acceptance

Kenneth A. Beavers, Ph.D.

GP

Galloway Press
Columbus, Ohio

Self-Worth
Without
Self-Worship:
The Bible-Based Approach
To
Self-Acceptance

By Kenneth A. Beavers, Ph.D.

Published by:

GP Galloway Press
1520 Old Henderson Rd., Suite 100
Columbus, Ohio 43220 U.S.A.

Copyright © 1995 by Kenneth A. Beavers. Printed in the United States of America

"Scripture taken from the HOLY BIBLE, NEW INTERNATIONAL VERSION.
Copyright © 1973, 1978, 1984 International Bible Society. Used by permission of
Zondervan Bible Publishers."

Publisher's Cataloging in Publication

Beavers. Kenneth A.
   Self-worth without self-worship : the Bible-based approach to self-acceptance / Kenneth A. Beavers.
   p. cm.
   Includes index.
   Preassigned LCCN: 94-076801.
   ISBN 1-883660-39-4

   1. Self-esteem--Religious aspects--Christianity. 2. Self-acceptance--Religious aspects--Christianity.   I. Title.

BV4647.S43B43 1994   158'.1
                                  QB194-1277

Cover design by Chad Planner
LCCN 94-076801 $9.95 Softcover

Foreword

Self-Esteem —

This is Ken Beavers' favorite topic and one of mine. He has spent most of his adult life helping people understand, accept and enjoy one of the most important gifts that God gives: a new sense of self-worth.

As a psychologist, Ken is excellent; as a teacher, he is insightful and helpful; as a student of God's Word, he is dedicated, committed, and literate. All those attributes taken together enable Ken to write a thoroughly Biblical and impressively helpful book for those who are searching for self-esteem or who find themselves helping others.

I have always been amazed that some pious, godly Christians emphasize the awful notion of self-rejection or even self-hatred. Scripture seems to clearly show the importance of each human being created in God's image, yet many preach a pernicious and damaging blend of gnostic self-denial and Christian language which is especially harmful to those who were abused or neglected as children. Only a person <u>with</u> a self has a self to give away.

Ken's thoughtful insights into Scripture and human thinking make this book especially redemptive and restorative to those damaged by toxic teachings and damaging relationships.

My own experience as therapist in the LifeWay clinic is that over 90% of our patients have been physically and emotionally abused. The result is a shattered sense of self and an overwhelming sense of guilt and shame. The truth of God does, however, set us free; and I see evidences of freedom from past rejection and trauma every day. The gospel is the <u>Good</u> <u>News</u>. In the midst of great darkness and enormous pain, God has called special people to deliver life and light. You are to be congratulated for getting and reading a book that, if you take it to heart, will deliver you the good news of a new mind and a redeemed esteem.

Gary Sweeten
Pentecost, 1994

Contents

Dr. Kenneth A. Beavers
C/O Galloway Press
1520 Old Henderson Road, Suite 100
Columbus, Ohio 43220

For information on the treatment programs
and workshops offered by Dr. Beavers write
to the above address.

 **Galloway Press**

Other books by Dr. Kenneth A. Beavers:

A Self-Esteem Guidebook:
Learning to Embrace Your Imperfect Self

Your Mental Mythology:
100 Lies That Shatter Self-Esteem

Chapter 1
THE BALANCED VIEW OF SELF-ESTEEM

"Stupid." "Jerk." "Lazy." "Pig." With what names do you punish yourself with when you fail? When you make a mistake? Or when you gaze at yourself in the mirror? If your self-talk is self-condemning, then you suffer from the most common form of self-centeredness. It's call low self-esteem. It is self-centered because while you are focused on your own defects, consumed by your shortcomings, then you will have less time to consider the wants and needs of those around you. While fearful about what others are thinking of you, you won't have time to worry about how others are hurting. While seething inside over someone's critical remark, a symptom of low self-esteem, you have less time to reflect upon reconciling with the criticizer. If you fear others getting to know the real you, again an outgrowth of low self-esteem, then you burn up energy hiding behind a false, inhibited self. Low self-esteem, shame, excessive guilt, self-hatred—a tremendous and destructive place of pain—is not where God wants you to be.

The Bible tells us, ". . . there is no one who does good, not even one" (Psalm 14:3). So how are we to feel about ourselves? God's Word commands us to ". . . not think of yourself more highly than you ought, but rather think of yourself with sober judgment"

(Romans 12:3). So what should our self-concept be like? But if, on the other hand, you are "fearfully and wonderfully made" (Psalm 139:14), then how should you care for yourself? If you are redeemed by God's only Son and are now called a child of God (1 John 3:1), then you must be a life with great value. So what should be the proper level of your self-esteem?

The Debate

There is an anti-self-esteem movement afoot in some arenas of contemporary Christian literature. Writers such as John MacArthur[1] and Jay Adams[2] consider themselves to be "Biblical counselors." Biblical counseling is defined as therapy in which the Scriptures alone are used to impart comforting and helpful information to a troubled individual. A *Christian* counselor is one who additionally draws upon the wealth of knowledge from the behavioral sciences including some traditional psychotherapy techniques. Both MacArthur and Adams appear to limit the scope of their counseling efforts to exclude the application of traditional therapeutic strategies that are easily consistent with scriptural teachings. MacArthur, especially, implies that using elements from traditional psychology in Christian counseling is a statement that Christ is not sufficient to meet our needs. MacArthur's and Adams' antipsychology arguments become especially heated regarding any notion of Christians needing to address the issue of self-esteem. Jay Adams, particularly, appears to emphasize human beings as being essentially valueless. Adams even goes so far as to say that people who are suicidal have too high a self-esteem. That is just the opposite of my clinical experience with suicidal patients who almost invariably consider themselves to be worthless.

Self-Worth Without Self-Worship

As a Christian psychologist, I have no difficulty integrating many aspects of the science of psychology with scriptural truths. The same is true for many other Christian counselors such as Joanna and Alister McGrath[3]. In fact, the melding of scriptural truths in carefully administered psychological therapeutic strategies lends a powerful mode by which to minister to a variety of hurting and bewildered members of the flock. I consider Christian psychotherapy to be a ministry and a personal calling. This ministry includes, and sometimes emphasizes, the need for hurting individuals to challenge elements of his or her own self-hatred. If enhancing self-esteem by acknowledging your heirship with Christ and your giftedness through the power of the Holy Spirit is what helps to decrease your depression, then this is exactly what must be done. If, for example, rejecting the lie that you must always defend yourself (another symptom of low self-esteem) reduces tension and conflicts in your marriage, then that is what you are called to do.

Let's say you come to see me to help you stop smoking. Jay Adams might suggest that I remind you of Christ's sufficiency in our lives and that your smoking habit is a sin which defiles the temple of the Holy Spirit. This is a scripturally-sound approach which could be enhanced by other psychotherapy techniques. If, for example, I guide you through some systematic behavioral strategies such as change of routine and self-reinforcement, your chances of successfully quitting the cigarettes increase. Thus, engaging in a counseling method which supports scriptural truths by adding elements of the science of psychology can be most beneficial. Going one step further, let's say you come to seek counseling for your severe depression. You believe that you are an utter failure in life in spite of much good evidence to the contrary. Let's say you also believe that the abuse you experienced as a child was your fault. As a counselor, I would help you to see the erroneous nature of your self-condemning beliefs which would result in a decrease in your self-hatred. Since improving someone's self-esteem is an effective treatment for depression, then your depressed state is likely to improve as you move from low self-esteem to self-acceptance.

Treating the lie-based self-disdain from which many people suffer is a psychological strategy that can solve many emotional and interpersonal problems. Helping an individual to gain self-acceptance is not only a potent treatment strategy, but one that is fully consistent with the Scriptures, as we shall see. For me to fail to minister to needy people with the fullness of my psychology education would be to neglect a direct calling from God. This would be tantamount to a physician having access to antibiotic medication but standing idly by while someone dies of an infection. If my helping you toward self-acceptance decreases your desire to commit suicide, then that is exactly what I must do. If your moving away from self-condemnation improves your ability to serve others, then that is precisely what you need to do.

Scripturally-consistent, traditional psychotherapy should not be rejected out of hand. Christ may choose to heal you through a physician's antibiotic. Christ may also choose to deliver you from a conflictful marriage by using someone with a knowledge of the behavioral sciences to help you see how your own self-critical style makes you hypercritical of your spouse. (For a more detailed summary of the debate between Biblical and Christian counseling, see: A House Divided?).[4]

Self-Worth Without Self-Worship

At a far different position are those who are fully caught up in the "self-esteem movement," especially those with so-called "New Age" ideas. New Age philosophy holds that humankind is evolving into a god-like form with limitless potential and an ability to find all solutions within the self. Exaltation of the self above all else is a primary belief for the New Agers. The notion of an external, omnipotent God is rejected since all-sufficient, god-ness lies within each person. New Age theology does not reject psychology but rather adds concepts such as "enlightenment" and special psychic powers. New Age theology is counter-scriptural to the point of blasphemy. Obviously, the exaltation of the self is not what God wants for us.

So where do we stand in the controversy which on one hand emphasizes the valuelessness of people and rejects any psychotherapeutic technique that seeks to increase self-esteem, and on the other hand, espouses the notion of man as God? I believe that, as in most things in life, there is a place of healthy balance. If low self-esteem feels so awful and yet the Bible condemns self-love (2 Timothy 3:1-2) and we are called to not esteem ourselves above others (Romans 3:9, Philippians 2:3), how should we then regard ourselves? The place of balance is one of truth-based *self-acceptance*. For the Christian, freedom from the pathology and prison of low self-esteem means that we reject the lies about ourselves that originate with the father of lies. A place of peace with who we are comes about first by knowing who we are in Christ. This results in the health and inner peace that is part of our heirship in Him. Self-acceptance empowers you to be in a greater place of ministry to which you were called by God and in a position where you are less likely to hurt others through possessiveness, jealousy, bitterness, competitiveness, etc. The pain of low self-esteem causes self-centeredness. Self-acceptance leads to decentering and allows you to be appropriately other-focused. Self-acceptance is the goal, and accordingly you should reject all notions of self-love, self-worship, or in any way esteeming yourself above others. Self-acceptance is not arrogance. It is, rather, a quiet and more realistic conceptualization of yourself including your position regarding God and your fellow human beings. Let us learn to use what we know to reject the sickness of non-scriptural self-condemnation. Let us know more fully who we are in Christ, not only loved by God but valued by Him as important tools in His service. That is what true self-acceptance is all about. At the same time, let us remember our neediness, our fallen nature, and our insufficiency apart from God. That is also a part of true self-acceptance.

We are neither worthless nor are we God. But those suffering from low self-esteem often believe the lie that they are worthless unless they behave as infallibly as God. Scripturally-based self-acceptance is the answer.

What is Self-Esteem?
Self-esteem, very simply, is the way you feel about yourself. Self-concept is different in that this represents your total knowledge of yourself, for example, how old you are or what you do for a living. Self-esteem is emotional, self-concept is intellectual. Feelings are more powerful than thoughts. The way you *feel* about how old you are is more potent than your simple knowledge of your age. Your *feelings* of competence in your job is more salient then your awareness of your job title. Self-esteem is critical, perhaps your single most important psychological need. If you don't feel good about yourself, you don't feel good. Low self-esteem, or self-esteem that is fragile is like exhaustion, everyone feels it some of the time but

some people experience it virtually all of the time. And like exhaustion, low self-esteem can affect everything you do and even dictate what you avoid doing. Without your being fully aware, low self-esteem can drive many of your behaviors and inhibit others. With low self-esteem you may be driven to perfectionism, leading you to overwork or to fear failure to the point where you don't even try. Low self-esteem is a distorted view of self in which you easily recount past mistakes yet fail to notice your strengths. Self-disdain can make you envious, self-conscious, bitter, depressed, and even suicidal.

Low self-esteem forces you into extremes. You may apologize too much or never apologize. You might persevere beyond reason or give up too easily. Low self-esteem makes you self-focused and self-conscious, while at the same time forcing you to incessantly fix other people's problems because you believe this is where your total value lies. Low self-esteem may cause you to brag in order to compensate for suspected defects in self, or low self-esteem may cause you to constantly put yourself down in front of others.

Low self-esteem can cause you to take everything personally, to accept abuse, and to be lonely. It haunts you, lies to you, and blinds you. Low self-esteem can ruin your relationships, force you into jobs that you hate, and cause you to be self-defeating. Later we will see how very many problems can be caused by low self-esteem and how pervasive a problem this may be in your life and in the lives of those around you. Non-self-acceptance is miserable.

Can You Identify?
Typical to cases I see in my office, was Linda, a 43-year-old divorcee who was depressed. Depressed for

so long, in fact, that she lost sight of what it was like to feel normal. In her mind, a natural part of living was to drag herself out of bed each day and force herself through eight hours of a dead-end job that simultaneously bored and frustrated her. She blamed herself for her failed marriage even though her husband was an alcoholic and even though she had done her best to keep the marriage alive. She believed that she was stupid and incompetent though her job performance would indicate otherwise. Linda believed that she was entirely unlovable and could not identify a single redeeming feature to her character. This, in spite of the fact that she is a pleasant, honest, and generous individual. Her parents had told her that she was stupid, her husband lived as though booze were more important than she was, and she attended a church which emphasized her lowly sinful state while negating the place of grace and redemption in her life.

Linda's pitifully poor self-esteem had caused her to remain in an abusive marriage far past the point of any reason. Her low self-esteem was central to her depressed state. It made her so self-conscious she was afraid to seek a healthier church, and consequently she remained distant from God. She did not have the confidence to realize that there were other jobs out there for her in which she would have been competent and happy. She felt unattractive and unappealing and, as a result, she was lonely.

Though not selfish, Linda, with her low self-esteem, was self-centered. She was so self-conscious that she seldom spoke up and when she did, she would later privately berate herself for saying the "wrong things." She believed that she needed to constantly prove herself on the job and thus was overly focused on how others were evaluating her performance day by day.

Self-Worth Without Self-Worship

Linda concentrated not so much in caring for others as much as she did in pleasing others lest someone reject her, or lest she be criticized for saying "no" to a request. Linda's low self-esteem interfered with her ability to be empathetic because she worried that she would not sound wise in her counsel.

Linda's self-view was so distorted that she would immediately dismiss any compliment that came her way, however accurate and sincerely delivered. Over criticisms, however, she would brood for days. She measured herself not so much by who she was but by her latest performance. She had trouble believing that even God could love her and for years had been spiritually stagnant.

Over the course of several months of therapy, Linda learned the keys to self-acceptance. She found out that in order to be acceptable she did not have to be perfect. She learned that it was okay to sometimes say "no" and even have other people disapprove of her. In a more balanced view, she recognized the gifts that God had given her—her generosity, her honesty, and her sympathetic heart. While not being the smartest person in the world, she realized that the messages that she was stupid, with which she grew up, were lies. By giving herself permission to sometimes say the wrong thing, she became less self-conscious about always having to say the right things. Linda came to understand that her value as a child of God came not so much from doing, but simply from being. By moving away from self-hatred, Linda was becoming better able to accept God's grace in her life and she approached her personal walk with Him with new enthusiasm.

Linda's depression lifted. She stopped smoking and she made several new friends. She now has a new job that she finds challenging and energizing. She gained the confidence to seek out what God had in store for her. I was privileged to watch Linda not only become healthier emotionally, but to mature as a woman of God. She joined a new Bible study and subsequently changed churches. It was fascinating to see her grow both in Bible knowledge and in the application of those truths in her life as she saw herself in an entirely new light.

Linda still struggles. As a single mother she worries about her children and continues to be strained financially. However, there is a new lightness about her. She has shed the cloak of self-dislike. She has reached the place of greater peace with who she is and what God intended her to be.

Self-acceptance comes about by your honest acknowledgment of who you are, both your gifts and your weaknesses. Self-acceptance allows you to let go of the burden of comparing yourself with others, needing to criticize others in order to hold yourself up, and competing with others in order to continually "prove" something. Self-acceptance is moving from lies into truths. It is going from sickness into health. From disturbance to peace. Having self-acceptance is not putting on the cloak of pride. Rather, it is shedding a cloak of self-denigration and self-focus. *Self-acceptance is seeing yourself as God sees you and seeing yourself as God would have you see yourself.*

Self-Worth Without Self-Worship

About This Book

This book offers you the tools to overcome the true psychological scourge—low self-esteem. As with Linda, addressing any emotional or relational turmoil by gaining self-acceptance can promote for you a new avenue for healing. Your work life, physical health, and even your spiritual life can be greatly changed through the increased peace of true self-acceptance.

In the next chapters you will learn more about the costs of low self-esteem and the potent benefits of ridding yourself of troubling self-doubt. You will begin with a detailed measure of your self-esteem. Then you will learn new ways out of what we call the achievement trap and the approval trap. You will gain insight into the torment of perfectionism and develop skills to change unhealthy thinking into balanced self-acceptance. There will be questions to answer, personal writings, and new behaviors to try. More than just a book to *read*, it is a book to *do*. Work through the book diligently. Seek to know much more about how God loves you and prayerfully discover a new view of yourself based on what He sees in you.

Your self-esteem is the problem. God is the answer. Self-acceptance is the gift.

The Balanced View of Self-Esteem

1.   John MacArthur, Jr. <u>Our Sufficiency in Christ</u> (Dallas: New Word Publishing, 1991).

2. Jay Adams, Christian Counsel <u>An Interview With Jay Adams</u> (Covenanter Witness, 1992).

3. Joanna and Alister McGrath <u>The Dilemma of Self-Esteem</u> (Wheaton, IL: Good News Publishers, 1992).

4.   Gary R. Habermas, Ph.D. <u>A House Divided?</u> (Chicago: Christian Counseling Today, 1993) Vol. 1, No. 4.

Chapter 2
SELF-ACCEPTANCE FROM GOD'S TRUTH

The Foundation

The Word tells us that, ". . . if anyone is in Christ, he is a new creation; the old has gone, the new has come" (2 Corinthians 5:17). The foundation for true self-acceptance must be based in the ultimate of truths, that is God's Word. And the truth is, that God deems you a *saint* (Ephesians 1:1). That's right, if you are a believer in the Lord Jesus Christ that means you are a saint. Not after you die, not when you remove all sin from your life, but right now. Jesus Himself never called anyone a sinner. The problem is, however, that we fail to see ourselves through the same eyes in which God sees us. Those of us who struggle with low self-esteem have failed to recognize the fullness of our heirship with Christ and are blinded by lies.

The blindness from which we suffer occurs as self-condemnation and keeps us from truth. Somehow, many of us feel more righteous in putting ourselves down and casting our identity in the dimmest possible light. Yet, this false humility flies in the face of your true identity as a believer. For example, ponder for a moment the fact that God considers you to be His child (John 1:12). God has communicated to you that you are an object of His love in the perspective of a parent caring for and protecting His most precious creation. Christ Himself considers you to be a fellow servant and

21

friend (John 15:15). You are now viewed by God as being holy and dearly loved and as being part of God's chosen people (Colossians. 3:12). So valued are you that you were bought at a price (1 Corinthians 6:20). And so important a vessel of God's that Christ Himself is in you now (Colossians 1:27).

The truth is, your low self-esteem leads you to disbelief in God's own Word. Rather than resting in the peace of the truth that you have become a new creation, you denigrate yourself by calling yourself names and continually trying to prove your worth. You live as if your value is based on perfectionism, pleasing other people, achievement and success, and generally playing all the right roles in life perfectly on cue. Many of us are caught up in activities that are motivated by what other people will think of us and generally struggle with self-doubt so that we not only diminish ourselves but also inadvertently extinguish the truth as given to us through the writers of the Scriptures.

You have become a child of God through your own belief, by grace which is freely given unto you. But with low self-esteem you feel driven to earn, to do, to excel, and to become perfect through your own strength and means. Your strivings, which are almost always an overcompensation for low self-esteem, rob you of the peace and abundant life promised through Jesus Christ. God's grace, which has made you a saint, was both a display of His love and indeed a testimony of your value in His eyes. Unworthy? Yes. But never worthless.[5]

The Scriptures are replete with themes that help underscore your true value. First of all, Christ was sent for you. The sacrifice of the Son, God's own beloved. We must also be valued by God since He

22

chooses to use us as His instruments of peace. He uses people like you to serve others. When you stop to think about it, how much of the time when God has heard your prayers has He used others to deliver you—a physician to aid in healing, a friend to listen, to comfort, to advise, or the good message of a pastor?

We are so valued by God that He cares about the very details of our lives. The hairs on our heads are numbered and He tells us directly that we are more valuable to Him than the rest of His creation such as the sparrows and the lilies of the field. Themes of God's compassion and deliverance are highlighted in the Old Testament in the lives of such characters as Abraham, Moses, and David. They were children of God just as we are. God values us enough that Christ, even at this moment, is interceding for us. And after He left, Christ cared enough to send us the Comforter, God's own Spirit.

According to God, He values us so much that Christ's second command is that we should care about and edify each other. God has made us in His image, with the capacity for compassion, discernment, and as spiritual beings. We are valued by God such that, ". . . he has given us his very great and precious promises" (2 Peter 1:4).

Unfortunately, it is my experience in working with people suffering from low self-esteem that it is simply not enough to remind them of God's love for them and their value in His eyes. It is almost as if their self-disdain outweighs their ability to let God's truth soak in. For most of them, low self-esteem seems to be a stumbling block which causes blindness. Addressing your need for self-acceptance can open your eyes to new truths that were there all along, resulting in new behaviors, attitudes, and ministries. In other words, a more complete expression of "the new creation" would occur.

Low self-esteem is built on such a foundation of self-deception that it can become almost impossible to reconcile yourself to all of the above truths. Therefore, self-acceptance can be a route toward a new openness to what God has to say. Coming to a place of peace with yourself can free you to accept all of the holy peace which is God's will for your life. Much is to be gained by shattering the sickness and distortion of unfettered self-doubt.

The Price of Low Self-Esteem
Self-esteem is so fundamental to your psychological make-up that most emotional and relationship problems can be linked to it. Part of the difficulty is, however, that when you're suffering from low self-esteem you seldom recognize its full negative impact in your life. It is critical, therefore, for you to learn to make self-esteem interpretations. That is, become skilled at discerning which of your stresses and fears in life have their bases in chronic self-doubt.

At the heart of making self-esteem interpretations is the understanding that much of what you do or even fail to do is in the interest of protecting your self-esteem or an attempt to raise your self-esteem. Here are some examples. Carol, who is a homemaker and a mother of two young children, occasionally finds herself screaming at her kids and saying things to them that she promised herself that she never would. Carol seems to explode at her children most angrily when they defy her authority. Though she does not realize it, Carol is taking personally her children's defiance and receives their rebellion as a personal insult. This effect is magnified by the fact that Carol already has doubts about her abilities as a mother. The threats to Carol's already low self-esteem cause such strong reactions in her that even she doesn't know where all the feelings come from.

Bill's low self-esteem controls his behavior in another way. As the owner of a small company, he is overcontrolling, domineering, and disliked by most of his employees. He almost seems to have a need to lord it over others so as to showcase himself as "the boss." Making other people feel bad seems to be Bill's way of helping himself to feel better about who he is. A man who is truly at peace with who he is would never have a need to treat people in such a way.

Our final example is Cheryl. Though married, her children are grown and she frequently finds herself longing for closer friendships with some of the women in her church. Additionally, she would like to volunteer as a helper for the children's youth program on Sunday nights. But Cheryl is so afraid of saying the wrong thing and of being rejected that she neither seeks out friendships nor follows through with her yearning to work with children. She justifies her inaction by telling herself that she is "just too shy." In fact, it is Cheryl's huge internal well of self-doubt that causes her paralysis. What little self-esteem she has, she carefully protects by taking no chances on being received negatively by others or by failing to be "good enough" in any new endeavor.

Carol, Bill, and Cheryl all have one thing in common. They are not self-accepting. They overreact, overcompensate, or become stuck in life as a result of their need to feel better about who they are. Their relationships are infected, their emotions often seem irrational, and their behaviors are heavily controlled by the pain of self-doubt. Learning to make interpretations regarding their self-esteem could greatly help each of our three characters understand what powers most of their reactions.

In what ways do you think elements of low self-esteem affect your actions? How self-conscious do you feel around other people? On what do you procrastinate out of fear of not doing well? Does perfectionism ever get in the way for you? How does it affect you when you are criticized? When you fail? Look at your actions and interactions, and especially your overreactions. Do you ever question why something made you so angry or caused you to feel so hurt? How much of what you do in life is in the interest of achievement in order to compensate for feeling insignificant? How many of your actions are in the interest of gaining the approval of others or avoiding disapproval?

Problems From Low Self-Esteem
Below is a list of some of the problems that are usually caused by low self-esteem. Note which ones are familiar to you.

Indecisiveness	*Excessive worry*
Fear of failure	*Feeling crushed when*
Stuffing your anger	*criticized*
Anxiety	*Exploding in anger*
Resentment and bitterness	*Depression*
Being easily hurt	*Perfectionism*
Overreacting	*Feeling jealous*
Feeling Stupid	*Feeling very angry at*
Shyness	*yourself for mistakes*
Inability to say "no"	*Loneliness*

Self-Worth Without Self-Worship

Focusing on your past mistakes and failures
Comparing yourself with others
Fearing disapproval
Taking things too personally
Failing to get close to others
Being overly "nice"
Irritability
Calling yourself names
Trying to be in the spotlight
Noticing only your flaws
Inability to relax or "goof-off"
Feeling driven to overachieve
Having vague life goals
Poor self-care
Needing to control others
Very low tolerance for mistakes
Placing excessively high demands on yourself

Not trusting your own judgment and decisions
Excessive worry about what others think
Putting your performance before relationships
Fearing rejection or anger from others
Allowing others to hurt and exploit you
Procrastinating
Blaming and fault-finding
Compulsive or addictive behaviors
Being overly cautious
Self-destructive/self-defeating behaviors
Turning your work into a "pleasureless drive"
Feeling inferior to others
Being highly critical of any project you've done
Having marital/sexual problems

Believe it or not the above is only a partial listing of the many kinds of problems that can be related to low self-esteem. Did any of them sound familiar to you? Do not be discouraged if you noted that you have experienced many or even most of the above concerns. Low self-esteem is nearly a universal problem and the above issues are extremely common.

In the interest of learning how to interpret life's issues through self-esteem eyes, can you identify how each of the difficulties in our list can be caused by the agony of self-doubt and in turn help perpetuate low-self esteem? For example, the problem of indecisiveness is worse with low-self esteem because you may be so afraid of making a wrong decision and looking foolish that you simply do not decide at all. Self-esteem is involved in many marital problems because with low self-esteem, feelings are easily hurt, people can become possessive and jealous, and one partner may have a need to dominate and control the other. Low self-esteem causes a multitude of problems, makes other problems much worse, and generally adds to the pressures and strains of everyday life. Learn to interpret your activities, your feelings, and your relationships with others, in light of not only your need for self-acceptance but that same need in the people around you. Self-esteem interpretations can clear up many mysteries and make the irrational seem more logical.

Low Self-Esteem and Sin

Low self-esteem contributes to your sinful behavior. For example, when you don't feel good about yourself, you are likely to have more difficulty in the management of your anger. Because of self-doubt, a person with low self-esteem is going to be more defensive and touchy and generally more irritable around others. Because of a strong need to protect self-esteem, overreacting to perceived threats becomes more likely and exploding in anger is often the result. Others, with excessive guilt caused by their low self-esteem, may never allow themselves to admit that they are angry even though there may be good reason for their anger. As a result, they may become passively aggressive by, for example, using sarcasm and other disguised methods of anger expression. Still others

28

with low self-esteem may have so much resentment and envy of others that bitterness and unforgiveness is always present.

Low self-esteem can result in the poor treatment of others. Being judgmental of others and using gossip are examples. People who don't feel good about themselves are often driven to reflect upon others in inferior light in order to boost their own self-evaluation. In likewise fashion, those who have not come to a place of self-acceptance may be locked in a constant game of one-upmanship or a competitive need to dominate others. Even abusive people are driven by an overcompensation for low self-esteem. This can occur when a person feels so insignificant that they ease their self-loathing by completely controlling and essentially squashing another human being.

People with low self-esteem engage in other sinful behaviors such as the self-doubting man who compensates for feelings of inadequacy with alcohol. Other compulsive behaviors, such as sexual promiscuity, are usually directly linked to elements of low self-esteem. Sexual acting out is usually a matter of needing to feel accepted, attractive, and desirable by another human being as much as it is a response to pure sexual desire. In fact, the drive for self-esteem is more powerful than the sex drive. Other sinful behaviors include lying and any action in which you may engage that is in conflict with your Christian values. For example, let's say you frequently get drunk with your co-workers after hours even though you do not feel right about doing this. With low self-esteem, you may not have the self-confidence to stand alone as a nonconformist out of fear of being labeled as weird or prudish.

Finally, low self-esteem distances you from God. Some people feel so worthless that they feel they cannot even approach the throne of God, even to repent. Still others, especially those who believe that their value is tied up in achievement, try to earn their salvation. Others fail to heed God's calling for humble service out of an irresistible desire to seek the accolades of man. Still others, when suffering from low self-esteem, are crushed under the burden of self-induced guilt, wrongly believing that God is condemning them for every mistake and failure from their past. Such people often assume that God hatefully judges them in the same way that they hate themselves. Thus, low self-esteem can cause you to limit God, doubt His grace in your life, and fail to accept His unmerited gifts and mercy.

Low Self-Esteem and Pride

As we have seen, many difficulties, including a number of problems of sin, result from the oppression of non-self-acceptance. The basic problem is one of *pride*. Pride is not high self-esteem or arrogance as we typically think of it. Pride, rather, is the same thing as low self-esteem. Pride comes about through self-doubt as one tries to overcompensate by becoming excessively self-sufficient. This self-sufficiency can even exclude your dependence upon God. Pride is a result of needing to say, "No thank you, Lord, I can handle it." Pride is a self-focused need to see yourself as being above others as well as being strong enough to control your life through your own will rather than God's. A need to feel superior can only spring from a hidden fear of being inferior. Jesus himself was particularly concerned about this problem. He addressed the apostles who were arguing about who would sit in the highest place and be seen as the greatest. Jesus said, "If anyone wants to be first, he must be the very last, and the servant of all" (Mark 9:35).

Self-Worth Without Self-Worship

I believe that Jesus knew that the person who was truly at peace with who he was would not need to overcompensate in a prideful manner. Jesus also knew that the self-accepting individual was more likely to be a better servant—gentler, and more willing to build up those around him or her.

In this way, we can see that the opposite of low self-esteem is not arrogance. You can also see that improving your self-esteem does not result in pride. Pride results from failing to address your problems with low self-esteem.

The Picture of Self-Acceptance

So what does the truly self-accepting person act like? How does he or she feel? What do they do differently? Socially, the self-accepter is willing to take social risks and express who they genuinely are. They are less concerned with what other people think, and as a consequence, more boldly conduct themselves as they believe God wants them to. They do not base their worth on the opinions and moods of those around them. Self-accepters also do not insist on being in the spotlight and receiving praises from others. They can focus on how others are feeling rather than how others are evaluating them. Making a good impression shrinks in importance compared to making a difference for someone else. Generally, high self-accepters are free to let others disapprove of them.

There are other positive ways that people with a high level of self-acceptance treat the people around them. Since these folks are more at peace with themselves, they are free to better use their energy for serving others. They can do this without making their own generosity the sole measure of their worth and without "sounding a trump before their alms." They can show a healthy balance between giving to others and seeking rest and time out for themselves. This self-care, which can better occur in the absence of low self-esteem, ultimately makes for a more consistent and giving caretaker for others.

High self-accepters have come to realize that they do not have to prove anything by controlling or winning out over others. Since they are more comfortable with who they are, they can be followers as well as leaders. They realize that others may not always do what they ask or expect and do not receive other people's reactions as a personal affront. Their self-esteem is not based on being top dog.

Other features of high self-accepters include the rejection of a need to harshly judge themselves and other people. They do not live with false beliefs that they are irredeemable and destined for ultimate punishment. The self-accepting person is comfortable leaving issues of punishment and judgment up to God.

The self-accepting person is able to recognize his or her own gifts and strengths. They utilize their talents with thanksgiving to God rather than seeing their entire worth as being tied up in those gifts. They know that simple acknowledgment of positive attributes is not the same as pride. The person with a good level of self-acceptance does not debase his or her own accomplishments, but instead openly recognizes God's willingness to work through him or her.

The self-accepter does not become bound up with worldly definitions of success and societal standards. Materialistic wealth and external signs of achievement are no longer measures of self-worth. The high self-accepting individual sees the need for God's grace in his or her life and has let go of the need to try to earn His mercy.

In general, seeing yourself as God would have you see yourself is part of the liberty that comes about through being a Christian. While the above description may be somewhat idealistic, it is worth progressing toward as you mature into the fullness of God's manifest love in your life and the abundant life promised through Christ.

Basic Premises
This book is designed to help you come to a place of greater self-acceptance and be released from the binding lies of low self-esteem. The book is based on a number of important premises.

1. The first premise is that you are an individual who has great value in God's eyes. While unworthy to receive His grace and mercy, you are certainly not worthless.

2. Your value was given to you while God formed you in the womb. Thus, you cannot earn your value, nor can you lose it.

3. God underscores your value by His action and mercy toward you and His use of you in His service.

4. Low self-esteem is a place of sickness and impairment. It is not part of God's original design that you should move through life burdened and impaired.

5.　Low self-esteem causes many problems in all areas of life. Some of these problems include self-destructive habits, destroyed relationships, and excessive drivenness toward achievement and approval.

6.　Low self-esteem is a form of self-centeredness. Low self-esteem is a place of pain, and when you are in pain you are too focused on yourself to adequately give to others.

7.　Low self-esteem is based in lies. All people with low self-esteem struggle with false beliefs. They may, for example, believe that their behavior must be perfect or include great achievements in order for them to measure up and have value in the eyes of God.

8.　Self-acceptance is the proper goal for improving self-esteem. Concepts such as self-love and self-worship are inconsistent with the Scriptures and must be rejected.

9.　Self-acceptance should be between you and God. Self-acceptance does not come about through achievement or the approval of men.

10.　Self-acceptance is a good thing. Self-acceptance is the opposite of pride since pride is actually an overcompensation for low self-esteem.

11. Self-acceptance makes you a better servant. Unfettered by the pain of self-hatred, you are freer to meet the needs of those around you.

12. Self-esteem can change. It is important to keep in mind that although you may have struggled with low self-esteem for many years, you can come to a place of healthy self-acceptance given a little time and effort.

13. Self-acceptance is a place of viewing yourself the way God views you.

14. Self-acceptance is how God wants you to view yourself.

15. Self-acceptance is an important component in the life more abundant as promised by Christ.

How is Your Self-Esteem?

How would you estimate your level of self-acceptance? What kinds of problems has low self-esteem presented for you throughout your life? What things about yourself do you have the most trouble accepting?

Let's now do a more formal measure of your self-esteem. Below are 48 statements. Mark each one as it applies to you in terms of how you feel about yourself today. Answer honestly. If a statement could go either way (or is sometimes true and sometimes false), ask yourself if it is *generally* true or false about you.

T	F		
—	—	1.	*I am not worried about looking old.*
—	—	2.	*I basically like the way I look.*
—	—	3.	*I don't compare my looks with others' looks.*
—	—	4.	*I think that I am sexually attractive.*
—	—	5.	*I believe that I am fairly intelligent.*
—	—	6.	*My judgment is as good as most people's.*
—	—	7.	*I can generally hold my own in discussions.*
—	—	8.	*I usually make intelligent decisions.*
—	—	9.	*I do not feel that I deserve punishment.*
—	—	10.	*I seldom feel guilty for things I have done.*
—	—	11.	*I have made no more mistakes than most people.*

—	—	12.	Mistakes I make do not greatly bother me.
—	—	13.	I am generally competent in my work.
—	—	14.	I approach most projects with confidence.
—	—	15.	I usually make good decisions.
—	—	16.	I have at least an average number of capabilities.
—	—	17.	I am not easily embarrassed.
—	—	18.	I am not self-conscious when friends are in my home.
—	—	19.	I speak up as much as anyone in a group.
—	—	20.	I am not shy.
—	—	21.	I seldom think about my personal flaws.
—	—	22.	I am not excessively sensitive to criticism.
—	—	23.	There are very few things about me that I desire to change.
—	—	24.	My imperfections do not greatly bother me.
—	—	25.	I am able to take care of my daily physical needs.
—	—	26.	My health is generally good.
—	—	27.	I am as physically strong as most people my age.
—	—	28.	I am able to get out and about as much as I used to.
—	—	29.	I have a strong sense of right and wrong.
—	—	30.	I am basically a moral person.
—	—	31.	I am generally fair when dealing with others.
—	—	32.	I seldom violate basic ethical principles.

— — 33. *I usually make my own decisions.*

— — 34. *I basically feel in control of my daily life.*

— — 35. *I am seldom around others whose moods affect what I do or say.*

— — 36. *I don't feel excessively controlled by my spouse or parents.*

— — 37. *I have made a difference in at least one person's life.*

— — 38. *If I were suddenly gone, others would experience loss.*

— — 39. *I have helped others and expect to do so in the future.*

— — 40. *I have contributed at least some small things in this world.*

— — 41. *I am not worried that I call on others too much regarding my problems.*

— — 42. *I seldom worry about wearing others out with my needs.*

— — 43. *I am not overly dependent on family to help me out.*

— — 44. *I do not feel like a burden on others.*

— — 45. *I feel that I am basically appealing to those around me.*

— — 46. *I think people would like me even if they knew me well.*

— — 47. *I am easy to like.*

— — 48. *I seldom worry about whether others will like me.*

Self-Worth Without Self-Worship

Scoring

A number of different factors contribute to your overall self-esteem. For example, your self-esteem is based on your perception of how intelligent you are, how attractive you are, how self-conscious you are, etc. Like most people, you probably feel okay about yourself in certain areas but not in others. Some of your separate areas of confidence may change from day to day, for example, following a compliment or criticism.

Self-esteem is a multifaceted characteristic. The way you feel about yourself is based on how competent or capable you are in your daily endeavors such as work, homemaking, parenting, etc. You also base your self-esteem on your level of morality or how much you feel you abide by your own sense of right or wrong. Having a sense of power is crucial to feeling in control of your daily affairs and being free to make your own decisions. Physical appearance is, of course, one aspect of your sense of self-worth, and so is physical capacity. Physical capacity has to do with your health being good enough to allow you to function and engage in basic self-care and to be mobile. You also privately evaluate yourself on your level of intelligence. The amount of guilt that you have and a sense of being burdened by past mistakes is also part of your self-esteem. Another factor is how much you feel you need to change in order to be satisfied with who you are. In addition, shyness or self-consciousness relates closely to your self-evaluation. Your impact, the positive influence you have had on the world around you, is another variable in your own private self-rating. The degree to which you feel like a burden on those around you can affect overall self-regard. Finally, you carry a sense of how appealing or likeable you are to others.

The above paragraph designates twelve variables that are components of your self-esteem. These factors are: *(1) physical appearance, (2) intelligence, (3) shame or guilt, (4) competence, (5) shyness or self-consciousness, (6) satisfaction with self, (7) physical capacity, (8) morality, (9) power or control, (10) impact, (11) sense of burdening, and (12) likability.* The 48-statement questionnaire that you just took has four items for each of these twelve factors. For example, items 1 through 4 measure your judgment of your physical appearance. Items 5 through 8 measure your self-rating of intelligence, the next four measures shame or guilt, and so forth. Take a pencil and place a bracket around items 1 through 4, 5 through 8 and so on, in groups of four to the end of the questionnaire. Beside each of those brackets write down the variable that each four-item group measures, using the above list of twelve variables.

Marking two or more items as false for any given variable is indicative of self-esteem problems in that factor. Do you have many separate areas of low self-esteem? Are there some factors on which you rate yourself positively? This formal measure of your self-esteem will enable you to highlight and refine exactly what kind of self-acceptance you maintain.

What findings surprised you from this evaluation? What do you consider to be your single most troubling area? Keep in mind your problematic areas as you work through this book.

Self-Worth Without Self-Worship

Some Food for Thought
Below are some important questions about your self-esteem and your daily life. Take some time to reflect on each one.

What does your low self-esteem cause you to do?
What does your low self-esteem prevent you from doing?
How does your self-esteem affect your relationships?
How does low self-esteem rob you of pleasure?
How does your lack of self-acceptance affect your relationship with God?
If you were more self-accepting, what would you do differently?

What To Do

1.   Answer on paper each question from the previous page. Give them plenty of thought. Be honest with yourself. Be thorough.

2.   Count the costs. As some of the above questions imply, low self-esteem can rob you of pleasure and interfere with your relationships. What price has been exacted from you because you are not fully self-accepting?

3.   Count the benefits. What would the peace of true self-acceptance mean to you? What changes could there be in your life?

4.   From the list of low self-esteem problems, which are the three most serious for you? What are the three most problematic areas you found from the self-esteem measure? Keep these concerns fully alive and in the forefront of your mind. Catch yourself manifesting these problems in your day-to-day work and interactions. Change begins with awareness.

5.   Describe some ways that pride has been an issue for you. That is, how have you overcompensated for your own self-doubt? For example, do you try to impress others, do things with perfection, or demand self-sufficiency from yourself?

6.   What are your goals in reading this book? Pray to the Lord that you would derive only what He wants you to learn and change in accordance with His will. Work hard and expectantly watch for answers to this prayer.

7.   Memorize and meditate on the full implications of this Scripture: "How great is the love the Father has lavished on us, that we should be called the children of God! And that is what we are!" (1 John 3:1).

5. For a more thorough discussion of learning who you are in Christ see: Neil T. Anderson <u>Victory Over The Darkness</u> (Ventura: Regal Books, 1990).

Chapter 3
THE ACHIEVEMENT TRAP

Rob wept. In the middle of the service, sitting at the end of the pew next to his wife and two sons, he buried his face in his hankie and shook. Though he was embarrassed, he could not stop the flow. After twenty years of attending the same church, Rob had only recently come to the realization of the true presence of Christ in his life. Rob recommitted his life to the Lord. Over the past year, Rob had begun to review his life and accomplishments. He thought about his success, the promotions, and his enjoyment of "the good life." He was depressed. Rob was unable to shake a gnawing sense of meaninglessness in all he had accomplished.

And so he cried. Rob cried because even though he had achieved everything that he had ever dreamed of, he was left feeling hollow and utterly dissatisfied. He cried because he had been driven by an insatiable need to succeed, a drivenness he barely understood. He feared for his marriage which was strained by years of neglect and too many late hours at the office. He wept for his two sons who were teenagers now. Most of the little league games, the fishing trips, and the school programs Rob had missed. He wept for years of fatherhood that he could never get back.

Rob had "arrived," but he felt like he was nowhere. He "had it all" but feared he really had nothing of true importance. By most people's measure, he was a success. But somehow Rob felt disappointed and empty. Only after reinvesting in the Lord did Rob's grieving become fruitful. He found happiness through rediscovering his love for his wife. He backed off from his hours at work for the sole purpose of spending more time at home. He got to know his sons again and did what he could to make up for lost time with them. At age forty-four, Rob turned his priorities upside down and finally discovered what success really means.

Self-Acceptance Versus Achievement
A lot of us are like Rob. Perhaps, for you, it is not necessarily success in the business world that you are after, but like many, you may be saddled with an unexplained drive to do more, be more, have more. We unconsciously believe that the more we accomplish the better we will feel about ourselves. Low self-esteem is once again a powerful controller of behavior that pushes us beyond all reason. Without realizing it, we have a sense that if we could only earn that degree, make this much money, lose so many pounds, or gain prominence and prestige, we would become more acceptable.

You will fight tooth-and-nail to avoid feeling insignificant and inferior. People will go to the extreme to prove that they are acceptable. This includes, as in the case of Rob, the sacrifice of the self, a marriage, and parenthood. Rob was not motivated by money, he was motivated by a need to feel better about who he was.

Gaining achievement is one of the most common ways that people try to raise their self-esteem. In what ways are you driven by a need for accomplishment? How much do you move forward in life because you are afraid to fail? What sacrifices have you made in the name of success?

Trying to gain self-acceptance through accomplishment is, at best, inefficient. People who are self-accepting do not need to drive themselves. People who are at peace with who they are do not push themselves to prove their value. It is critical to know that no degree of accomplishment will ever increase your worth. It is liberty to know that no failure will ever diminish your value. Jesus Himself said, ". . . a man's life does not consist in the abundance of his possessions" (Luke 12:15).

Trying to gain self-acceptance through accomplishments simply does not work. In fact, success may have the effect of lowering your self-esteem. But how can this be? Think for a minute. When you finish a project and step back to look at it, what do you mostly notice? The flaws, right? If you already suffer from low self-esteem, no achievement is enough. You will note only the flaws and remind yourself that you could have or should have done better. You also likely play the comparison game, wherein you measure your own successes against the achievements of others. This habit, more often than not, leaves you with a sense of coming up short. Additionally, without being at a place of self-acceptance, you will tend to diminish your own accomplishments anyway. "Well if someone like me could do it, it must not have been that difficult in the first place."

Success is just not satisfying. An accomplishment almost never feels as good as you might have hoped or expected. Though you try to earn a sense of self-worth, you are left feeling flat. One way to know that the drive for achievement does not lead to self-acceptance is to ask yourself, in the course of your life, how has it worked so far?

An unhealthy drivenness can come in many forms. Cindy had three young children. Her husband worked full-time and she worked part-time while taking on most of the responsibilities for the care of the house and the children. She sewed her children's clothing, always had meals on time, and yet was never late for work. Cindy could not shake the feeling that she was never doing quite enough. She asked of herself to do more and more. She served on committees at church, and took on extra duties at work. She drove herself to meet every need of her family even to the point where she tried to anticipate those needs in advance.

Cindy learned to ignore her own needs. She was exhausted most of the time and almost never took time out for herself. She was so busy throughout the day, she barely took the time to go to the bathroom or to eat a decent meal. Cindy was not really happy, but she couldn't slow down. Her own insecurities and self-doubt drove her on. Deep within, she sensed that success at home and at work would help her to feel better about herself. She lived in fear of failure, powered by a dread that her self-doubts were well-founded.

A Pleasureless Drive

Rob and Cindy were both caught up in what is called the *pleasureless drive*. This is the endless and unhealthy effort to gain achievement and success. It is a drive born out of a need to feel better about yourself, and it becomes pleasureless since you will suffer almost anything to gain self-acceptance. The pleasureless drive can leave you tired and self-neglectful, as in the case of Cindy, and disillusioned, as with Rob.

Hidden within the pleasureless drive is a phantom goal that is called the *point-of-arrival*. This is a mythical place of award or reward or a sense of having "made it." If you are driven to achieve, then it is almost certain that you base your self-worth on whether or not you reach this point-of-arrival. For some, the point-of-arrival is to make vice president of their company. For others it is having perfectly happy children. For some it may have to do with certain material possessions or a specified salary. What is your personal point-of-arrival? What is the criterion upon which you have been basing your own sense of self-acceptance? In what ways has your own pleasureless drive robbed you of true meaning and happiness? Are you overly busy and too tired? Do you feel stressed and strained much of the time? Does what you do in life just never seem to be quite enough?

The Lies
How is it that we become caught up in the pleasureless drive? Why do we base our sense of worth on reaching a point-of-arrival even though it doesn't really exist? If self-acceptance is based in truth, then non-self-acceptance must be based in lies. What are some of the false things that you believe that keep you driven to somehow earn your worth?

First of all, you may believe that you are saved by your works. Though most of us know that we are saved by faith, many of us still carry around a sense that we have to *do* well in order to gain God's approval. We often forget what Paul taught us in Ephesians (2:8-9), "For it is by grace you have been saved, through faith—and this not from yourselves, . . . so that no one can boast." God designed it so that His love and mercy would be our saving grace, not our own efforts and success. God's love is to be highlighted, not our ability to accomplish. It is best to think of yourself as having been saved *for* works rather than *by* works.

The nonscripturally-based belief that you must earn God's acceptance becomes translated into a sense that you must earn your own acceptance. In this way, rather than accepting yourself just as you are today, flaws and all, you perpetually try to like yourself more by piling up accomplishments. Just as it is unnecessary and doesn't work with God, so will it not work for you.

Other lies that we believe about our accomplishments have to do with the ideas that you must always be in a state of self-denial, and that all of your behaviors must be altruistic. Many people are professional "pleasers," constantly finding themselves in the role of making everyone else happy even to the detriment of their own health and well-being. Some people feel that the only proof of their worth is in what they can do for others. Other lies have to do with your accomplishments themselves. You may erroneously believe that only your efforts which are painful and costly count for anything. Anything that comes easily to you somehow doesn't count. You may denigrate any of your accomplishments, thereby denigrating yourself. You may feel like an impostor because you sense that everyone around you knows more and does more than you do. You may also be caught up in the lie that in order to be worthwhile you must be productive virtually all of the time. Perhaps you think that if you do not do your best every minute of every day and thus reach the fullest of all of your potential, then you have failed.

Self-Worth Without Self-Worship

Deep down, maybe you believe that if you are not great at something then you amount to nothing.

Lies about failure also can contribute to your pleasureless drive. Perhaps you believe that when you fail you *are* a failure. It is important to keep in mind that you are not your behavior. Your behavior is simply one of many expressions of who you are. Some people are absolutely terrified of failure and carry a deep sense that failing proves inferiority and thus must be avoided at all costs. Even Paul felt like a failure at times (Romans 7:15).

Which of the above lies have infiltrated some of your thinking? If you let go of some of these lies, how much closer to self-acceptance could you become? If you were able to see your failures as God sees them, how different would be your self-talk whenever you fail?

The truth is that you are saved by your faith and not by works. If you accept yourself as God accepts you, then your self-esteem should have nothing to do with your lifetime balance of success and failure. The truth is, you do not have to prove yourself. You cannot be productive at all times and it is unhealthy to try to be. The truth is, most of us are never great at anything and, in fact, most of us are just average at most things we try to do. Self-denial, altruism, and pleasing others must be seen in balance with self-care (Philippians 2:4). The truth is, you will never reach your full potential. The truth is, failure doesn't prove that you are inferior, and failing doesn't make *you* a failure. Often, failure, because of outside influences, doesn't really say anything about you at all.

Success

Let's take a closer look at this thing we call success. What is it that we are trying to achieve, anyway?

The modern American definition of success basically includes what the Bible calls the storing up of earthly treasures. If you were to ask a group of people what they would consider success to be, you would hear notions of material wealth including cars, homes, and plenty of money in the bank. Additional elements of the traditional definition of success also might include fame and influence. This kind of success can be winnowed down to "the five P's"—Power, Position, Prominence, Prestige, and Possessions. Success means plenty of each of the P's.

The problem is that most of us have bought into this worldly definition of success. Without fully realizing it, society defines our worth and low self-esteem drives us to attempt to gain worth. Though many of us could intellectually say that we reject such worldly ideas of success, we still find ourselves measuring who we are by such a nonscriptural definition.

The problems with defining success according to the above standards are multiple. Again, success generates a drive to reach certain points-of-arrival with a drivenness based in untruth. "They exchanged the truth of God for a lie, and worshiped and served created things rather than the Creator—who is forever praised" (Romans 1:25).

The worldly definition of success leads to competition. This competition pits man against his brother and establishes a system in which there are few winners and many losers. This kind of success gives rise to envy and jealousy. The Bible tells us that the love of money is the root of all kinds of evil. And as Jesus spoke of the rich man entering the kingdom of God as being like a camel going through the eye of a needle, He showed that seeking success can keep you from God.

The lower your self-esteem, the further you are away from the peace of self-acceptance, then the more likely it is that you will adopt a worldly, nonscriptural definition of success. When your self-esteem is low, you will attempt to do whatever you can to raise it, including the storing up of earthly treasures. But it never works. Even highly successful people can struggle with very low self-esteem. Celebrities, professional athletes, and other people who seem to have truly made it are often no closer to being at peace with who they are than we common folk might be. Success is not the answer. The best way to reject a worldly definition of success is to become self-accepting. In this way, your self-esteem is not based on outside worldly measures.

What We Really Want
The biggest lie about success is that it promises to take you somewhere, and that *somewhere* is a place of peace with yourself. But success, in the worldly sense, fails to deliver. Here is what people really want: people want a sense of peace and satisfaction with themselves and their lives. People want rest and they need comfort. As you are caught up in the pleasureless drive, it is likely that what you are really seeking is meaning and purpose. What people long for is affiliation, or a sense of belonging and being a part of others' lives. What people search for is justification for their being and a sense of impact or the feeling of making a difference. In other words, the real search is not so much for success as it is for self-acceptance. True success does not come about by gaining worldly

53

things and having great accomplishment. True success is not *having* to have these things.

Notice that it is quite possible to have many elements of traditional success and none of the peace, meaning, and sense of satisfaction that you really seek. Notice also that it is possible to find purpose and peace in the absence of having any worldly success. One set of desires is independent of the other. Success may not lead to satisfaction and meaning in life but true self-acceptance can. You cannot be at peace unless you are first at peace with who you are.

This is not to say that self-acceptance takes preeminence over God in your life as the One who gives deepest meaning, justification, and purpose. Knowing God is the source of all peace and comfort. Following Christ can give rest and a sense of satisfaction like nothing in the world could ever do. However, in the absence of self-acceptance, you will never be able to fully embrace these many promises from God. How can you accept His love if you feel unlovable. A myth abounds that says you cannot love anyone else unless you first love yourself. This is not true. People with very low self-esteem can easily love others. It is only in the receiving and the acceptance of love from others where they get into trouble. How can you sense God's forgiveness if you are troubled by an abiding belief that you are unforgivable? How can you accept God's calling to service if you fail to acknowledge your own gifts and strengths and are paralyzed by the fear of failure? How is it possible for you to trust that God values you if you constantly tell yourself that your value lies somewhere within the five P's?

Self-Worth Without Self-Worship

Self-acceptance is the goal. It is necessary for you to embrace the new creation that you have become (2 Corinthians 5:17), to reject the pattern of the world and to be transformed (Romans 12:2).

What To Do
Do you find that the "pleasureless drive" describes some aspects of your life? Are you reaching for some phantom point-of-arrival in order to attempt to shut off feelings of insecurity? Do you try to raise your self-esteem through some worldly definition of success? Can you admit that achievement is one of the ways that you strive toward self-acceptance? If so, there are a number of things that you can try. Listed below are a number of thought-provoking suggestions upon which you will want to take some time to reflect or even write out on paper.

1. The first thing to do is become aware. So many of our actions are long-standing habits and we lose sight of our true motivations. Think about and perhaps jot down some of the ways in which you are caught up in worldly definitions of success and the ways in which you try to raise your self-esteem through accomplishment. How could the term "pleasureless drive" be connected with your life? Which of your strivings are you becoming aware as being in the interest of managing your self-esteem? If you were at the place of true self-acceptance, what would be different in terms of your goals and strivings? What things do you need to tell yourself so as not to be caught in chasing unrealistic points-of-arrival?

2. Count the costs. You will become more resolved to give up the idea that achievement will help you feel self-accepting when you bring into question

the burdensome nature of your strivings for success. In other words, if you realize the problems that have been caused by your attempts to succeed your way to self-acceptance, then you will be more motivated to drop old bad habits. What have been the costs to your relationships? Examples here might include loneliness, neglect of relationships, divorce, etc. What have been some of the possible costs to your physical health? Some examples may include neglecting medical needs, insufficient rest and relaxation, chronic fatigue, etc. What have been some of the costs to your emotional well-being? Some potential costs include depression, anxiety, stress, addictions, etc. What have been some of the costs to your outlook on life? Some examples here may include dissatisfaction, disappointment, burnout, many regrets, etc. What have been some of the costs regarding your self-esteem? Some examples here may include being overly focused on your failures, disappointment in yourself, perfectionism, feeling worthless, etc. What have been some of the costs to your relationship with God? Some potential problems here include being too busy to hear His call, neglecting to grow in the faith, failing to accept His grace in your own life, pride that is based on works, etc.

3. Develop your own definition of success. Consider the absurdity of the standard,

worldly definition of success and decide to reject it. Think about what it is that you *really* want from life and what is truly important to you. Then, take some time to contrast what you really want from life with what you have spent your time chasing. Also, take a closer look at what God wants you to do. You may find that His will for your life does not include some of which you have been killing yourself over.

4.   Strive for balance. Think about what you would need to add to your life and to take away in order to gain balance. Balance means finding reasonable time to give to pleasure and rest as well as to work. Balance means giving as much priority to relationships as to performance.

5.   Let yourself become fully convinced that trying to gain self-acceptance through achievement does not work. Finish the sentences below.

> *My attempt to increase my value through achievement is ridiculous because...*
> *Some of my pleasureless drive behaviors are...*
> *My attempting to prove my worth is self-destructive because...*
> *My seeking achievement does not really help me because...*

58

Trying to be successful may conflict with God's will for my life because...

6. Count your potential blessings. Consider how different your marriage might be if you didn't spend time trying to accomplish things. What might happen in some of your friendships if you were not overly busy? Think about some of the things that you would like to do that you just don't take time for. Consider how good it might feel to be well-rested. Reflect upon the fun that you could have. Think about the spiritual growth that you might enjoy if you were not always striving for earthly things.

7. Become aware of and reject the lies that have bound you to the need for achievement. Which of the lies from earlier in the chapter sounded familiar to you? What are some healthier alternative ways of viewing yourself and your purpose in life?

8. Make some simple changes in your behaviors. Rather than endlessly and doggedly slaving away in the chase for success, try some of the following:

    Remove some needless task from your life. For example, don't vacuum the house twice a week when once a week might suffice.
    Learn to say "no" sometimes.

Give something or someone you love
some extra attention.
Slow down, learn to do one thing at a
time.
Stop and take time out for rest.
Build into your schedule times for
vacation, relaxation, and self-care of
body, mind, and spirit.

9.   Make a comparison between your values
and where you spend your time. In
other words, if you list out your
priorities, and at the top of the list are
church and God, and you realize you
only give one hour a week to your walk
with the Lord, then something is out of
sync. If you decide that your family is
more important than work, but you
never see your family because of your
work, then it may be time to make
changes.

10.   Make some decisions right now. Decide
to stop comparing your achievements
with the achievements of those around
you. Stop self-criticizing and second-
guessing every accomplishment and
failure. Do not diminish your accomplishments. Enjoy them with thanksgiving without making them the basis for
your self-esteem. Decide to seek self-
acceptance rather than success. Decide
that right now is the best time to begin
to make a real change in your life.

11.   Memorize and reflect upon this
Scripture: "For it is by grace you have

been saved, through faith—and this not from yourselves, it is the gift of God—not by works, so that no one can boast" (Ephesians 2:8-9).

Chapter 4

THE APPROVAL TRAP

The Approval Problem

What if you woke up tomorrow morning and no longer cared at all what anyone ever thought of you? What would it be like for you if you suddenly had no fear of anyone's disapproval or dislike of you? What if you *truly* did not care what others thought? How would your life be different? What would you do differently? What would you wear? What would you say?

The approval trap, something with which most of us struggle, is an even more potent driving force in our lives than the need to achieve. We need to be liked. We strive for approval. We recoil from criticism and disapproval as if they were electric shocks. We can't stand it when someone is angry with us or dislikes us. We conform, we comply, we even lie in order to stay on the approving side of the people around us. What of your behaviors are ultimately motivated by this nearly universal need to gain approval and avoid disapproval?

"I wish you'd stop asking me so many questions!" Margaret snapped at Sarah. Sarah was the personnel manager for a medium-sized computer company. She had only recently begun her job and was still learning the ropes, seeking help from people like Margaret, a secretary. Margaret's comment stung like a slap in the

63

face. Sarah could not stop thinking about it. She was
hurt and angry and wondered why Margaret did not
like her. Sarah absolutely hated it when someone
disliked her.

Sarah was the ultimate conformist, a veritable social
straw in the wind. She so much wanted to be approved
of by her peers that she changed personalities
depending on whom she was with. When she was
talking in a group that used bad language, Sarah swore.
She would join another group in office gossip, even
though it was unlike her to do so, because she feared
others would consider her to be a prude if she did not
chime in. Around other Christians in the company, she
bragged about her church life. But when talking with
her unchurched co-workers, she carefully hid the
spiritual aspect of her life.

Sarah's need for approval made what could have been
a very pleasant job a tense walk on a tightrope for her.
She'd become terribly upset over the slightest criticism
and brood about it for days. Whenever someone was
cool to her, she assumed that she was no longer liked
and became preoccupied with getting back into the
other person's good graces. Any meeting became a
tense ordeal. Full of good ideas, Sarah usually sat in
silence during the weekly staffings out of fear of
sounding stupid or, worse yet, offending someone.
Sarah longed to be noticed for her good work, but
dreaded even the slightest disapproval.

What Jesus Had to Say About It
The Word shows us a number of times how concerned
Jesus was with the issue of people being motivated by
the approval of others. Christ said, "Be careful not to
do your 'acts of righteousness' before men, to be seen
by them" (Matthew 6:1). "And when you pray, do not

be like the hypocrites, for they love to pray standing in the synagogues and on the street corners to be seen by men" (Matthew 6:5). "When you fast, do not look somber as the hypocrites do, for they disfigure their faces to show men they are fasting" (Matthew 6:16). Jesus was stern in his warning that the approval of men will avail you very little. Additionally, a preoccupation with seeking the accolades of those around can separate you from the love of your heavenly Father. "If you do, you will have no reward from your Father in heaven" (Matthew 6:1). "I tell you the truth, they have received their reward in full" (Matthew 6:5).

God desires that you be motivated by your worship of Him. He does not want you to exchange the temporal and earthly (worldly approval) for what is eternal (heavenly reward). As illustrated in our example with Sarah, your heavenly Father knows what a wasteful and stress-inducing use of your energy it is to want everyone to like you.

What About You?
In what ways do you worry about what others think of you? Consider areas of competence, appearance, and your character. Also, consider various settings where you may be worried in this way, such as in the work place, in your home, at church, in public, etc. How does your concern over what others think of you control your behavior? How does it prevent you from being completely yourself? Can you think of a time when you did exactly what you did not want to do out of fear of what others might say? In what ways are you socially shy out of fear of what "they might think"? When someone obviously dislikes you, what do you say to yourself about yourself?

You can tell that you are motivated by seeking approval and avoiding disapproval if you feel deeply hurt by rejection or criticism. If you are overly self-conscious in public or easily embarrassed, approval is probably important to you. You also may be overly concerned with what others think about you when you realize that you sometimes say what you do not really mean or continually fail to express yourself, including your emotions and your needs. Have you ever noticed that any kind of exposure or scrutiny makes you extremely tense? Are you excessively worried about your appearance? Think about how careful you are to avoid disappointing those around you. Consider how strong your need is to impress others and have them like you.

Your need for approval has as its source your own self-doubt. Because low self-esteem is such an unpleasant feeling, you attempt to seek relief by using others' responses to you as proof of your value and worth. You are, in essence, telling yourself that if other people like you, then perhaps you're not as bad as you fear. The problem is that your striving for approval can exact a great cost from you. For one thing, you must conform to the ways of the world in your attempt to get the world to approve. This effort flies in the face of God's desire that you do not conform to the patterns of this world (Romans 12:2). We normally connect the term "peer pressure" with children and teenagers. However, peer pressure does not end in childhood. Unless you have reached a point of healthy self-acceptance, you will find yourself inexorably enticed by the positive strokes from your associates. These strokes are the proof that you unconsciously long for as evidence that you are a worthwhile human being.

The need for approval is part of the self-centeredness of low self-esteem. The self-accepting person is not preoccupied with his own image nor lost in the wondering of how he can stay in everyone's good graces. Your need for approval probably has its origins in early childhood. Like any child, you absolutely *had* to have your parents' approval. Without it, you were frightened, lost, and miserable. As an adult, you now treat everyone you know as if they were your parents. You want their love, you wish to please them, you want them to clap when you turn somersaults. In God's eyes, your value is unconditional. In your own eyes, your value becomes conditional based on the criterion of how people around you are reacting to you.

The Potency of Approval

In order to underscore how powerful can be our drive to meet with the approval of those around us, let's look at what happens to the victims of a religious cult. Cults are groups with religious overtones and usually a powerful, living leader. Cults are about the control of individuals. Low self-esteem of the victim paves the way for ensnarement in a cult. Manipulating the power of approval and disapproval gives the cult its bewildering strength to hold people captive.

Cults often seek out young people, especially those who are feeling alienated, isolated, and who have little social support. These individuals often have a vague sense of who they are, feel insecure, and confused (in other words, low self-esteem). A potential new cult member is befriended by those who appear to be caring and accepting people. Ready-made, approving friends are used as bait. Self-esteem is manipulated by shame as indoctrination includes interrogation, public confessions, and other experiences of intense self-criticism and doubt. Disciplinary action is swift and often uses guilt. Positive reinforcement is based on approval and comes in the form of smiles, praise, acceptance, and expressions of love. Cult members experience approval when they reject the outside world, and engage in complete sacrifice for and obedience to the cult leader. The young and insecure new cult member feels liked and accepted when he or she holds the leader's and the cult's beliefs in greater esteem then his or her own. For the new cult member, the need to be liked by others overrides critical, rational thinking. Filling an insecure person's need for approval can outweigh most other needs.

Approval Doesn't Work
Just as striving for achievements does not move you to a place of greater self-acceptance, neither does approval end your insecurities and self-doubting. For one thing, trying to get everyone to like you can be exhausting. You try to please this one over here, you strain to impress that one over there, you worry about offending anyone—all very tiring. In order to fit in with those around you, you may even "sell out" and violate your own moral or ethical standards, like Sarah in our example, who found herself gossiping with the rest. As a social chameleon (taking on the character and flavor of the person that you're with), you may end up feeling phoney. Your efforts to please, impress, and to fit in cause you to present a false self. Thus, any approval that you do receive may not be based on the real you. Therefore, you may dismiss it when people like you because at some level you are aware that it's not based on your real self. In fact, trying to gain approval may actually lower your self-esteem because you dislike yourself for being phoney and selling out.

If ninety-nine people really like you and one doesn't, and you are full of self-doubt to start with, guess of which person you're going to be most mindful. Trying to gain other people's approval to prove your own worth is doomed to fail because obviously not everyone will like you. Even if everyone did like you, you might find yourself wondering how much or if they would continue to like you if they knew you better. What is more, in your striving for approval, people do not always communicate clearly how they do feel about you. At times people may like you when you have assumed just the opposite. The bottom line is this: you will never be able to fundamentally change how you feel about yourself if your self-esteem is based on the whim and mood of people around you. The approval from others will never be enough. Your self-esteem cannot be based on external events, including the actions and attitudes of your family and peers. Your sense of self-worth must be unchained from empty applause and approval. Self-acceptance must be a separate and private matter between you and God, "So that it will not be obvious to men.....but only to your Father, who is unseen; and your Father, who sees what is done in secret, will reward you" (Matthew 6:18).

Lies of the Approval Trap

Just as with the achievement trap, if you are caught up in the approval game, then you are probably the victim of certain false beliefs. For example, somewhere inside, you probably believe that gaining the approval of everyone around you is a reasonable goal. Also, you may believe a lie about conforming, which tells you that it is crucial for you to fit in with the people around you. You may believe that your appearance has bearing on your value as a human being and this lie keeps you chasing after approval. You may also be caught up in the belief that others must agree with your ideas and opinions for them to be legitimate and worthwhile.

Other lies are related to disapproval. It is erroneous for you to believe that all criticisms of you are necessarily a reflection of who you are. Likewise with rejections. If someone rejects you, it actually may have little to do with who you are and more to do with the person who is rejecting you. It is false and destructive to believe that criticism, rejection, and other forms of disapproval must be avoided at all costs. Believing that you always have to make a good impression can cause unneeded strain. If you feel that you must always please others lest someone dislike you, then you are needlessly wasting energy.

Healthier, more truth-based beliefs include the notion that you will never be able to get everyone to like you and attempting to do so is a waste of time and energy. Your ideas and opinions are legitimate with or without the agreement of others. Conforming and fitting in is not always best and, in fact, the Word calls us to not conform to the ways of this world. Additionally, you would be better off if you were generally less concerned with always making a good impression and specifically did not care so much about your physical appearance. Furthermore, criticisms are as much a reflection of the person being critical as they are of you. (Handling criticisms will be discussed in greater detail later in this chapter.) Finally, keep this in mind. If some people disapprove of you and even dislike you, then you are probably doing something right.

Societal Standards and Expectations
The approval trap causes you to look toward society's standard rather than God's. The best illustration of this is to look at how Madison Avenue through television commercials spells out expectations that you must meet in order to be worthwhile. In your effort to avoid disapproval, you conform. These commercials, which

are effective because they manipulate your self-esteem, tell you that you must be:

> *young*
> *attractive*
> *thin*
> *financially secure*
> *popular*
> *problem-free*
> *sexy*

Furthermore, the media spells out in great detail what you must avoid in order to side-step disapproval. You are deemed worthless if you have any of the following:

> *gray hair*
> *bad breath*
> *varicose veins*
> *excess weight*
> *limp hair*
> *an old car*
> *out-of-date clothes*
> *static cling*
> *ring around the collar*

What all of this means is that in order to be approved of by man you must give superficiality priority over depth. Appearance must have greater importance than substance. Your image matters more than your character. All of this is, of course, the very opposite of what God asks of us. God cares little about your bad breath or limp hair but intimately wants to know the depths of your heart (Psalm 139).

Counting the Costs
Since the approval trap primarily has its effect in the social arena, most of the costs are to your relationships.

For example, because disapproval and rejection may be such a fearsome prospect, shyness and even social paralysis may result. You may be terrified of speaking up in groups. Or, you may make absolutely sure that you know where others stand on an issue before speaking your own opinion. This may result in your not saying what you really mean or otherwise failing to express your true self.

You can become so concerned about what others might think of you that you begin to mind read and over-interpret others' responses to you. In other words, you may make social mountains out of molehills by interpreting an innocent comment as containing some sort of hidden insult. Some people even go so far as to reject other people first in order to prevent being rejected themselves.

The compulsion to be liked can cause an individual to show off, brag, have a need to be in the spotlight, or to actively solicit approval and compliments. People sometimes wind up doing painful and expensive things to their bodies in order to improve their appearance. At its worst, people who cannot accept themselves and who demand the approval of others, end up hating their own bodies. The approval trap is one of the main roadblocks to self-acceptance.

The most important psychological consequence of the approval trap is the cost to your self-esteem. Basing your own sense of self-worth on whether or not others like you, can only lead to trouble. There are not enough people on the planet who can like you enough to truly cause lasting change to your fundamental sense of your own worth as a human being.

Self-Worth Without Self-Worship

Finally, there is a spiritual cost. Conformity to the ways of the world separates you from God. If you do not feel worthy in the eyes of others, there is a danger that you may feel ineligible to approach the throne of grace. As a result, you will have trouble receiving the fullness of God's mercy, truth, and life.

Pleasers

A significant human cost in the approval trap occurs when you become so fearful of disapproval that you wear yourself out pleasing others. In my experience with patients, this seems to be more a problem for women than for men. Many women play an overly "nice" role in life where they see themselves as *fixers*. These women are often most attracted to men who are extremely needy and demanding. A pleaser allows others to hurt and even exploit them. Because approval is so important to them, their whole identity and sense of self-worth is measured by the good things that they can do for someone else, especially a boyfriend or husband. These women are usually quite unassertive and have a deep sense that they do not deserve to be in mutually beneficial relationships in which love and attention are reciprocated. They become great caretakers to the detriment of their own needs.

Do you wear yourself out racing around trying to make sure everybody else is happy? Do you find yourself repeatedly in relationships that are unfulfilling or even exploitative? Do you feel that you have very little to offer in a relationship except to "fix" someone else? How much does your need for approval cause you to be a pleaser?

Managing Criticisms

Critical comments hurt. This is especially true when you work hard to avoid being disapproved of. How do you respond to a critical comment? Do you get angry, do you sulk, have you ever found yourself obsessing about a criticism for days or even weeks after it occurred?

Brooding about a criticism thrown your way is needless agony. In order for you to be truly self-accepting, you must gain a new perspective on criticisms. This is done in two ways. First, when you have been criticized, stop focusing on yourself and begin to think about the criticizer. Second, learn to criticize the criticism. Here's how.

In order to focus on the criticizer, learn to entertain hypotheses about that person. Let's say that Fred, a co-worker, tells you that you did a terrible job on some project. Rather than mentally reviewing all of the things that you should have done differently and kicking yourself for every imperfection, concentrate on Fred. Generate hypotheses about what it was in *him*, not you, that made him sound disapproving. Maybe Fred was simply in a bad mood. Perhaps he had a fight with his wife that very morning. Fred may just be a critical person, speaking harshly to everyone. He may have low self-esteem and, therefore, a need to put others down. Perhaps Fred is threatened by your good work and criticizes you out of his own fears.

The truth of your hypotheses is irrelevant. You may never find out if Fred had a fight with his wife that day, but as long as you focus on Fred you cannot spend time thrashing yourself. Focusing on the criticizer encourages you to take things less personally by contemplating other reasons for disapproval. Doing this is not the same as passing judgment on another. You keep your hypotheses private by way of contemplation in order to stop thinking about yourself.

Self-Worth Without Self-Worship

For many people, just the suggestion that a criticism may not be proof positive that they are totally incompetent, can provide relief. Focusing on a criticizer, the opposite of what you normally do, is a way to be less self-centered.

The second task in managing criticism is to criticize the critical comment itself. Before you reflect upon the possibility that a criticism may have some merit and even offer you a degree of potential benefit, it must pass certain criteria. An acceptable criticism must be:

> *Objective*
> *Potentially Helpful*
> *Educative*
> *Regarding Something Significant*
> *Sincere and Relevant*
> *Tactfully and Privately Spoken*
> *Clear*
> *Purposeful*

Unacceptable criticisms are usually unworthy of your worry and mental energy. Unacceptable criticisms tend to be:

> *A Matter of Taste or Preference*
> *Destructive*
> *Punitive*
> *Petty*
> *Character-Related*
> *Manipulative*
> *Harshly and Publicly Spoken*
> *Vague and Without Potential Benefit*

The next time a critical comment comes your way, measure it against our acceptable/unacceptable criteria. Do not pass judgment on a criticizer but do learn to be critical of any criticism. By measuring any critical comments against the above criteria, you further your efforts at releasing your fears related to disapproval. In this way, self-acceptance can be better separated from the acceptance you perceive from other people.

What About Compliments

How do you handle compliments? If you are like most people who have trouble with self-acceptance, you probably have noticed that your memory for compliments is far shorter than that for criticisms. Often, people get into the habit of discounting compliments when they come their way. They may question the sincerity of the person giving the compliment or think of some canceling flaw so that the compliment is no longer legitimate.

Begin to see your compliments as being a piece of research data worthy of your analysis. Think of a compliment as being a reflection of yourself from another person who does not carry the same "anti-you" biases that you carry. Learn to accept compliments graciously. Remember your compliments. Learn to say "thank you" and leave it at that. Learn to spend as much time contemplating your compliments as you habitually have your criticisms.

False Self/Genuine Self

As we have previously stated, trying to gain self-acceptance by gaining the approval of those around you can cause you to produce a false social self. This is actually denying who God designed you to be.

How do you know when you're not being genuine? If you never disclose your real self, or you tell others that you agree with them when you really don't, then you are not being genuine. Or you may find yourself saying what you don't really feel or think. Being disingenuous may cause you to force a false attitude, perhaps of nonchalance or unreal confidence. Maybe you are afraid to show your emotions. Do you ever lie or exaggerate about yourself in order to craft a false image? Are you aware, as we have previously described, that you are always trying to fit in, to conform, to go along with the crowd? You know you are being less than genuine when you are afraid to ever say, "I don't know." People who are pleasers are also putting forth a false image. You can tell that you are being less than genuine any time you use manipulations such as leaving hints rather then directly asking for what you want. There is something false if you never spontaneously express your real emotions, or if you always smile or make jokes when you are hurting inside. Being disingenuous means caring more about being proper than being sincere.

In a sense, we are all fakes. Some self-disguise is good. For example, we have all said that we were "fine" when actually we were falling apart on the inside. And certainly it would not be appropriate to lean over to the guy in the pew next to you and say, "Boy, does your breath stink," even if that would be a genuine opinion. But problems can come about by seldom or never genuinely expressing your individuality.

Decide now to be more genuine. Firmly resolve that a more full expression of your true nature is no longer to be avoided. Try to disclose more of your true self. Take a chance, speak up. The next time someone asks your opinion, tell them what you *really* think. Do something new that is self-expressive. For example, buy a piece of clothing because *you* like it, fashionable or not. Eat a weird combination of food. Tell someone a well-kept secret about yourself. If you are genuinely quirky or flawed, let others see some of that also. Be unremarkable, mediocre, and boring if you have to be, but be yourself. If you need to say it, say it honestly. If you are unhappy, stop painting that frozen smile on your face.

Jesus has asked us to let our "yes" be "yes" and our "no" be "no." When you are genuine, what people see is what they get—unadulterated and unfiltered, solid and sincere. Commit to telling the truth even when it is unpleasant to do so. Being genuine means sometimes saying, "I do not know the answer." It means sitting down when you are tired. It means crying when you are hurt. True self-acceptance can begin with delivering unto others the real you in accordance with God's wise design. (Learning to be genuine will be described in much greater detail in Chapter 13.)

Self-Worth Without Self-Worship

What To Do

There are a number of things that you should try in order to dislodge approval from others as a basis for self-acceptance.

1. Try the suggestions already mentioned in this chapter. The next time you are the receiver of a critical comment, generate some hypotheses about the criticizer and learn to be critical of the criticism itself. When you receive a compliment, use it as important, objective information about yourself and remember it. Also, practice being genuine as described in the last section.

2. Start challenging your own compulsion for approval-seeking. Ask yourself several questions. What is the worst that could happen to me if I did not fit in? If I disappointed someone, how bad could it be? What is the worst thing that could happen if I did not fulfill my usual caretaking role, just once? What is so awful about being disliked or disapproved of? Is disapproval so frightening that it must be avoided at all costs?

3. Count your own personal costs. How have your relationships been hampered by your need to seek approval? What energy and worry have you expended in the effort to avoid disapproval? What kinds of stress and anxieties do you incur as a result of your drive to be liked? In what ways have you become a

79

mind reader, an over-interpreter, or even paranoid? What kind of pain have you endured as a result of rejection or criticism? And finally, what efforts have been wasted in putting forth a false social self?

4. Write out a comprehensive paragraph answering one question. If I woke up tomorrow not caring at all what anyone thought of me, what would I do, stop doing, say, and wear?

5. Pretend that you truly do not care about what others think and actually behave as such. The next time you are around others, purposefully do not avoid disapproval and see how different you can be.

6. Think about and try to adopt the attitudes that a self-accepting individual would have about this issue of approval and disapproval. Here is a model to follow.
    High self-accepting people:

    *Express themselves in an open and
    genuine manner*
    *Take chances with being wrong, being
    embarrassed, and even being rejected*
    *Do not base their self-esteem on the
    opinions and moods of others*
    *Have no need to be the center of
    attention*
    *Do not need to solicit the praises of
    others*

80

*Are comfortable with the fact that some
people inevitably will not like them
Do not take personally everything that
other people do or say around them
Do not strive to be like everybody else
Are able to hear and enjoy compliments*

7. Become aware of your own tendency to be a "pleaser" or to "fix" people. Ask yourself if you believe that you have any value beyond your ability to make some specific person happy. Do you need to bring about change in some relationship in which you are being exploited? Do you need to be around people who are more likely to reciprocate in the giving of attention and love?

8. Learn to be critical of Madison Avenue and society's standards and expectations. That the media, especially television commercials, have anything to offer by way of measuring your true human worth is a lie. Begin to watch the media and advertising with a harshly critical eye. Learn to question the absurdity of society's messages rather than silently criticizing yourself for your inability to conform.

9. Firmly decide now to give other people permission to not like you and to disapprove of you. Take significant chances on being disapproved of and remember that if someone doesn't like you, then you are probably doing something right.

10. Contemplate your status as "aliens and strangers in the world" (1 Peter 2:11), and what it will take for you to truly no longer be conformed to the pattern of this world, but to be transformed (Romans 12:2).

Chapter 5
RENEWING
YOUR
MIND

As A Man Thinks

The Bible indicates in Proverbs 21:29 that who you are is in large part determined by the way that you think. But did you ever think about the way that you think about yourself? You cannot be entirely objective in the way that you look at and evaluate yourself. As you reflect upon the kind of person that you are, you will see yourself through a screen of defenses, biases, and distortions. Anything that produces a distortion in the way you see yourself takes you away from objective reality, or truth. King David knew that God wants us to seek and know truth about ourselves in a depthful way. In Psalm 51:6 David writes, "Surely you desire truth in the inner parts; you teach me wisdom in the inmost place."

Though you may not be fully aware at this point, the way you think about yourself is probably far from being reality-based. While most of us think that we have a reasonable and objective vision of who we are, we are saddled with a number of *thinking errors* that destroy objectivity. These thinking errors, rather than being specific beliefs, have to do with your "style" of thinking. For example, if you have a style of thinking which includes overall pessimism, then you are likely to maintain a certain critical self-view. If your style of thinking instead includes a tendency to always look on the bright side of things, then your internal picture of yourself may be quite different. The general style by which you think about yourself is determined by the number and kinds of thinking errors present in your habitual thought life.

Your goal is to learn about the kinds of errors in your thinking. As the name implies, thinking errors are not truth-based and therefore must be modified so that the way you think about yourself falls more in line with the way God thinks of you. In the next few pages we will begin to list and define a number of common thinking errors, some of which will probably feel familiar to you.

Thoughts and Feelings
Low self-esteem and self-acceptance are primarily feeling-based experiences. So why are we talking about the ways in which you *think* about yourself? The way your mind works is that thoughts affect feelings and feelings affect thoughts. If you think that no one could ever love you, then you will not feel very good about yourself. On the other hand if you feel depressed, then most of your thoughts are likely to center on gloomy topics. While thoughts and feelings interact with each other, it is easier to intervene in the way you think in order to change the way that you feel. Trying to change feelings directly is difficult. But changing your feelings, especially the feelings you have about yourself (your self-esteem) can come about by taking a hard look at the way that you think about yourself.

As we have stated, the problem is that the way you think about yourself is fraught with thinking errors. As long as these errors are present in your self-view, your thoughts will be negatively biased against yourself and your feelings will be unpleasant. In the presence of thinking errors, which almost always lead toward a negative self-bias, self-acceptance becomes impossible. Your thinking errors, however, have become habitual and even automatic. Distortions in your thought-life regarding yourself occur more frequently than you might think. For many people, chronic, negative thinking errors in self-evaluation have been around so long they seem normal and even objective.

Let's look at an example of someone whose self-view is full of thinking errors. As you get an inside view of this person's thought life, see if you can detect the distortions present in her thinking. Carolyn is a bright young reporter for Pittsburgh's main daily newspaper. She is well-liked by her co-workers and almost always seems to do a great job. However, Carolyn is never satisfied with herself. She is highly critical of her own writing and is unhappy that she never gets her stories "just right." She is also seldom comfortable while at the office. Carolyn thinks that she knows that other people at the office are dissatisfied with her work. Though she receives many compliments for her work, she believes that other people are simply not telling her what they really think. Because Carolyn does not see herself in positive light, she becomes easily discouraged. Once she did a story on homelessness that was rejected by the editor. Even after several rewrites, her story never ran. Carolyn concluded from this incident that she was and would probably always be a mediocre reporter.

Carolyn had a way of taking everything personally. If anything went wrong in the office, she seemed to dig around for reasons why it might be her fault. She became reluctant to take on difficult assignments in continual fear that she might blow it. Her internal dialog consisted of negative self-commentary and an ongoing wondering if other people noticed that she was not quite up to par.

Can you see the distortions in Carolyn's thought life? Can you imagine how she must *feel* about herself deep down if she *thinks* in this way? Does your personal thought life regarding the way you think about yourself reflect any similar distortions illustrated in Carolyn's story?

The Thinking Errors
When you endeavor to think more about your thinking and to begin to change it, it is critical to learn to apply labels to certain elements of your thought life. What we want to focus on is learning to detect and name certain distortions or thinking errors that probably have become automatic and, consequently, are outside your awareness. The thinking errors delineated in the next pages produce a negatively distorted view of yourself. While you can be defensive at times and fail to see some problem areas in your behaviors and attitudes, most people with a lack of self-acceptance tend to fail to see positive aspects in themselves because of their thinking errors. Your safest assumption is that you generally underestimate yourself and view yourself more negatively than is probably realistic. Habitual use of these thinking errors represents unhealthy thinking.

As you read through the list of thinking errors below, place a check mark by each one that sounds familiar to you. This will help give you a picture of your general thinking style. As you read through them, be aware that when you put some of your thought processes into words, they may seem absurd to you. So even if you intellectually disagree that you buy into a certain type of thinking error, ask yourself if you feel or behave as if you engage in that error.

Self-Worth Without Self-Worship

At this point you may be thinking that your view of yourself is entirely realistic and objective. But if you are suffering from any self-esteem related problems, you can be sure that there are negative twists in your self-evaluations and that you think of yourself with an overly critical eye.

We will look at ten thinking errors.

1. **Filtering.** Filtering is a tendency to focus on negative aspects of your self while disregarding the positive. It is as if your perceptual apparatus is surrounded by a mesh. This mesh has holes large enough to let in memories of your past mistakes and thoughts about your negative personal features. But the mesh acts as a filter that does not allow recollections of success and positive characteristics to come through. John Quincy Adams was quoted as saying the following: "I can scarcely recollect a single instant of success in anything that I have ever undertaken." This statement came late in his life after he had been a senator, a U.S. ambassador, and President of the United States. Like all of the thinking errors, if you engage in filtering you are probably not aware of it. Filtering for you may have become habitual and so automatic as to deceive you into believing that your negative way of viewing yourself is the only way that represents accuracy and objectivity.

2. **Personalizing.** Personalizing is the belief that negative responses by others

87

are a reflection of you. If you engage in personalizing and someone around you is in a foul mood, your first response may be to wonder what you have done wrong. Or, in another example, if someone forgets to phone you as promised, you may spend an inordinate amount of energy trying to figure out why they do not like you. People who personalize may try to take any socially negative occurrence and turn it into support for their well-established negative bias toward themselves.

3. **Pathologizing**. Pathologizing is the general belief that what you feel, think, or do is basically abnormal. If you struggle with self-esteem problems, you may be worried that a lot of your fleeting thoughts and fantasies are weird. You may tell yourself that you are crazy and abnormal whenever you feel any level of anxiety or depression. You apply subtle pressure to yourself to always be perfectly steady, consistent, and happy. Otherwise you may begin to tell yourself that there is something wrong with you and that you are not like other people. There is a general failure to recognize that we are all just a little crazy.

4. **Global Labeling**. Global labeling is the habit of using demeaning labels to summarize who you are. Typical labels include "jerk," "lazy," "fat," "stupid," or any other less-than-complimentary

slam. It is not uncommon to hear people summarize their entire personality with a single deprecating label with which they would never blast anyone else. These demeaning terms are used as if it were possible to encapsulate the complexity of an entire personality into a single word. What are some of the uncomplimentary names you privately lay on yourself?

5.   **What-ifing.** What-ifing is the entertaining of images of disasters, mistakes, and rejection. When you engage in this thinking error, you allow your imagination to run through the litany of every possible negative outcome. You may be quite adept at filing through a mental film strip of every possible mistake that you could make or opportunity for embarrassment in any given situation. "What if I say the wrong thing?" "What if they find out how little I really do know about this subject?" "What if I mess up in front of everybody?" "What if she doesn't like me?" "What if I lose?" "What if I tell him and he laughs at me?" "What if I am in an accident and I am not wearing clean underwear?" "What if...?" "What if...?"

6.   **Mind Reading.** Mind reading is when you assume that you know what other people are thinking. For example, Jim stops to rest for a moment at his machine just as the foreman walks by.

Jim is now sure the foreman thinks that he is "just a goof-off" on the job. Do you assume that you know what others think about you even when there is no real evidence to support your notions? Do you tend to read between the lines or over-interpret someone else's silence? Mind reading is a good example of why putting some of the thinking errors into words may seem absurd to you. If someone were to ask you if you can really read other people's minds, you would say that you cannot. However, you may go through life feeling badly because of your assumptions that you know what other people are thinking. Do you engage in some forms of mind reading?

7. **Editorializing.** Editorializing is the habit of constantly, privately commenting on your own looks, personality, and behaviors. When struggling with low self-esteem your editorializing is likely to have a strongly negative tilt. You may find yourself going through the day figuratively looking over your own shoulder. A lot of editorializing takes place while looking in the mirror. Another time in which you may find yourself engaged in this thinking error may be when you are evaluating some past performance. If you engage in editorializing, it is as if you are a stage player being shadowed by a theater critic who makes ongoing comment about your performance.

8. **Overgeneralization.** Overgeneralization is the tendency to draw a general conclusion about yourself based on flimsy evidence or a single incident. For example, you decide to go back to college and you do not do well in your first class. You then jump to the conclusion that you are not "college material." Or someone turns you down for a date and this becomes proof in your mind that no one would ever want to date you. If you engage in overgeneralization, your conclusions about yourself may seem to you to be clear, deductive reasoning. However, when struggling with low self-esteem, it is likely that you jump to premature conclusions that contain a slant that supports your already negative self-bias.

9. **Black-and-White Thinking.** Black-and-white thinking is the habit of seeing yourself in extreme, all-or-none terms. If you find yourself being unproductive, you call yourself "lazy." If you make a mistake in disciplining your child, you then conclude that you are a "failure" as a parent. You may believe that if you are not great at something that you are attempting to do, then you are a flop. With black-and-white thinking there are no gray areas. You are either completely successful or you are a total failure. You are either at the top of the heap or you are a nobody. Black-and-white thinking may cause you to fail to recognize that you, like everybody else,

are a mixture of pluses and minuses and that your characteristics, skills, and styles of interaction vary from day to day.

10. **Self-Second-Guessing.** Self-second-guessing is a tendency to constantly reevaluate your past decisions, behaviors, and plans. People who do a lot of self-second-guessing are frequently looking back rather than living in the present or planning for the future. The self-second-guessing usually takes place with an overly critical eye. Self-second-guessing is quite different than an objective post-analysis designed for information gathering in order to learn from past trial and error. If you utilize this thinking error, it is likely that you habitually list out ways in which you could have or should have done better in the past. This overuse of 20-20 hindsight is unfair and painful.

Did any of these ten thinking errors sound familiar to you? Do not be dismayed if you noticed that your thinking style includes many of these errors.

Take a minute to re-read Carolyn's story. See if you can now identify and label the kinds of thinking errors which troubled Carolyn and kept her from self-acceptance.

When you are, in any way, struggling with lack of self-acceptance, thinking errors tend to control your self-talk. Because of certain errors like editorializing or self-second-guessing, these distortions in your thought life perpetuate unrealistic standards. The thinking errors also make you think that you might be the only one—for example, the only one who messes up, the only one who becomes afraid, etc. The thinking errors narrow your self-perceptions, blinding you to your God-given gifts by helping you to focus on your defects. Generally, these errors in your thinking help to maintain the self-centeredness that comes about through low self-esteem. You have an increased memory for your failures and a greater tendency to make mountains out of molehills.

What To Do About It
Romans 12:2 calls you to "be transformed by the renewing of your mind." Since thinking errors are, by definition, distortions in perception, then to undermine these errors means to move closer to God's truth. Renewing your mind regarding self-perception takes place in three steps: (1) awareness, (2) challenges, and (3) replacement.

Awareness is key. If you are like most people, you have spent much time thinking but very little time thinking about your thinking. And when is the last time you identified and labeled your thoughts? After you have learned how to name the kinds of thinking errors in your view of yourself, you want to catch yourself using such distortions. Your awareness will increase as you learn to name the various kinds of thought processes that have automatically gone on in your mind. You can use some internal cues to tell you when to focus on your own thinking. For example, whenever you are feeling low or feeling anxious, ask yourself what you have been telling yourself. Check to see if you have been engaged in one of the thinking errors that you marked for yourself. Other cues to look for include feelings of discomfort that occur while interacting with others. Even sighing can be a cue because that behavior is often an indication that you are releasing some tension and it is therefore likely that you had some tense thought. Keep in mind that your thoughts flow in a logical chain of associations. Therefore, by linking each thought back to the previous thought, you can trail back in order to figure out what you were telling yourself in accompaniment to your unpleasant feelings. More often than not, when you do this you will be able to detect one or more thinking errors.

To enhance your awareness, learn to label your thoughts. In other words, when you catch yourself engaged in a thinking error, call it what it is. Then, talk to yourself about the way you talk to yourself. For example, you could say, "Well, I'm doing that thing called 'filtering'. I am once again focusing on the negative and disregarding the positive. I am also 'global labeling' because I just called myself some dirty names." Remember, you are trying to change lifelong habits of thinking styles and this will take practice. What you are doing is restructuring your internal tapes so that they will begin to say something more healthy. Repetition along with increased awareness is paramount to renewing your thinking style. When you increase your awareness, you may be surprised at how often you engage in thinking errors.

Challenges
Rather than being critical of yourself, you want to learn to become critical of your thinking style. There are several ways of becoming critical of your thinking errors and each of these methods is called *challenging*. When you challenge one of your habitually distorted ways of thinking, you bring a thinking error under

scrutiny so that it becomes clearer to you how biased and harmful that thinking error can be.

The quickest and easiest way to challenge your erroneous thinking is to present yourself with questions that bring into doubt the legitimacy of your thinking errors. In other words, you want to ask questions of your thinking style that highlight how harsh and unrealistic some of your self-distortions can be.

Below is a list of questions that you can begin asking yourself any time you find that you are engaged in one or more of the thinking errors. Making yourself answer some of these questions helps you to challenge some of your long held beliefs about the kind of person you are. Consider your thinking errors and ask:

1. *Am I confusing a belief with a fact?*
2. *What is rigid and unyielding about the way I am thinking?*
3. *What is distorted about this thinking error?*
4. *What are the burdens this thinking error places on me?*
5. *What is the evidence? Would that assumption hold up in a court of law?*
6. *How might my thinking be different if I were kind, gentle, and accepting toward myself?*
7. *Do these thinking errors solve any problems for me?*
8. *Am I using extreme language such as "always," "never," and "no one"?*
9. *How would I look at it if I were more self-accepting*
10. *How is this thinking error a roadblock for me?*

11. *What difference will it make a year from now? Ten years from now?*
12. *Who does it help for me to continue to think this way?*
13. *Who says so?*
14. *In what ways is this thinking error not leaving room for my human imperfections?*
15. *How might I be a more helpful, loving, and less self-centered person if I gave up this thinking error?*

We will look at an example of challenging a thinking error. Let's say that you engage in a lot of mind reading. Let's start to challenge by asking the first question, "Am I confusing a belief with a fact?" This challenge question helps you to see that you might "believe" that you know what other people are thinking but you cannot really count these assumptions as fact. You might also challenge by asking, "What is the evidence? Would that belief hold up in a court of law?" This challenge will help you to see that it is erroneous to base your feelings about yourself on the ideas that you project into other people's heads, rather than looking at hard evidence. Finally, you could challenge your mind reading habit by asking, "What difference will it make a year from now?" This challenge can help you realize that you may be worried about something, that even if true, really doesn't amount to much.

Learn to apply these challenge questions any time you are suspicious that you are using thinking errors. Some of the challenges work better for some people than others. Memorize a few that seem to work well for you and use them frequently. It is most effective when you not only ask these challenge questions but also come up with a full answer as it relates to your particular thinking error.

Another way to challenge your thinking style is to ask questions that encourage you to count the costs of distorted thinking. Think about the errors that you use a lot and then ask yourself some of the following questions:

1. *What are the disadvantages of thinking that way?*
2. *How does it hurt me?*
3. *How does it help me?*
4. *How does it limit me to use this thinking error?*
5. *How does it perpetuate false beliefs about myself?*
6. *How does it rob me of pleasure in life?*
7. *How does it decrease my level of self-acceptance?*
8. *How does it interfere with my relationship with God?*
9. *What is a more healthy and balanced way to view myself and my situations?*

Do the same things with these cost-counting challenge questions as you did with the other list of challenges. Use the ones that seem to work best for you.

Replacing the Errors
After you learn to identify your thinking errors and to challenge them, you will want to replace these errors with more realistic, truth-based thinking. Below is a list of self-statements that you can learn to say to yourself to help displace some of the distortions with which you view yourself. Several affirming, healthy,

alternative thoughts are presented for each of the thinking errors.

1.   **Filtering**.   Affirming alternative thoughts include:

I will allow myself to see both the positive and negative aspects of myself.

My negative self-bias is not founded in truth.

When I focus on the negative aspects of myself I do not see the whole picture.

I do not filter out other people's positive features, so I will no longer do that regarding my own.

I will begin to search for evidence regarding my own positive features.

God wants me to know the full truth about myself, and this includes seeing the positive as well as the negative.

2.   **Personalizing**.   Affirming alternative thoughts include:

Things that go wrong are usually determined by a variety of factors.

People often respond to me out of their needs and hang-ups, not out of anything I have done wrong.

Since I am only human, I cannot always prevent negative outcomes around me.

The way people respond to me is not entirely up to me.

I do not need to overanalyze my contribution to negative events around me.

I will seek God's wisdom about each negative situation in my life, rather than reflexively blaming myself.

3. **Pathologizing**. Affirming alternative thoughts include:

My feelings are legitimate and do not need to be justified.

Everyone is probably just a little crazy.

Even when my thoughts and feelings are difficult to understand, they are still legitimate.

I will let myself be a little "abnormal" at times.

Since "normal" is so difficult to define, I will no longer constantly strive for it.

It is more important for me to seek and be who God wants me to be, rather than attempt to be "normal" or like everyone else.

4. **Global Labeling.** Affirming alternative thoughts include:

I am too complex to summarize in a single word.

Applying a label to myself means that I am ignoring some other important features.

I will refuse to call myself names in the same way that I would not accept being called those names by other people.

Calling myself a name when I mess up just makes the situation worse.

Since calling myself names does not help anyone, I am going to stop that habit.

I will remind myself that even with my weaknesses, according to God I am still a child of His.

5. **What-ifing.** Affirming alternative thoughts include:

I will no longer respond to my fears as if they are already true.

I cannot really predict the future.

When I stop and think about it, most of my worst fears have never come true.

What-ifing means unnecessary suffering.

Living is risky but need not be feared.

Very few of my mistakes become true disasters.

It is better to be reasonably cautious than to worry about every possible negative outcome.

I will try to focus on Jesus' words which call us to be anxious about nothing but to think about our reliance on a loving heavenly Father.

6.   **Mind Reading.**   Affirming alternative thoughts include:

I have not been endowed with the power to read minds.

I will stop "reading between the lines" when interpreting other people's words and behaviors.

I will stop basing my own self-esteem on what I think other people are thinking of me.

I will learn to focus on evidence rather than my own assumptions about what is happening in other people's heads.

It is better to ask someone what they are thinking and feeling rather than act as if I already know.

I will learn to better rely on God's wisdom and discernment rather than my own error-filled assumptions.

7. **Editorializing.** Affirming alternative thoughts include:

Since most of my editorializing is negative, it is just another form of needless self-punishment.

I would not put up with someone else walking around with me all day commenting on all I do, so I will refuse to do it to myself.

There are much better ways of maintaining good performance than editorializing.

Editorializing prevents me from experiencing and enjoying the present moment.

I do not have to evaluate everything about myself and everything that I do.

If God is accepting and forgiving of my mistakes and shortcomings, I will learn to have those attitudes toward myself.

8. **Overgeneralizing.** Affirming alternative thoughts include:

Jumping to a conclusion about myself almost always leads to a negative self-evaluation.

A few regrettable behaviors are not sufficient to draw a conclusion about who I am.

Any negative overgeneralizations are simply unfair expressions of my low self-esteem.

Jumping to a conclusion about who I am is just another way of putting myself down.

I will learn to focus on God's conclusions of me which include the fact that I am chosen of God, holy and dearly loved.

9. **Black-and-White Thinking**. Affirming alternative thoughts include:

I will stop placing myself and my personality characteristics in either-or categories.

Most human features are on a continuum from good to bad, high to low, or strong to weak.

Most things in life need to be viewed in shades of gray rather than being completely black or all white.

It is impossible for me to be all bad and ridiculous for me to strive to be all good. Black-and-white thinking limits my perspectives and my choices.

I will remember that God's way of thinking about me has left room for error, weakness, and shortcomings.

10. **Self-Second-Guessing**. Affirming alternative thoughts include:

Self-second-guessing is just another way of being self-critical.

Lamenting my past decisions does not help me as much as deciding to make amendments and adjustments in the future.

Being critical of past decisions and behaviors is far too easy, yet destructive. I do not reevaluate everyone else's past decisions and behaviors so I will stop doing it to myself.

I will learn to model God's thinking, which includes grace, forgiveness, and a letting go of my past mistakes.

In looking at the affirmative alternative statements above, is there a contrast between those statements and the way that you habitually talk to yourself? How did it make you feel as you read through the affirming statements? How would things be different for you if you believed to your very core the things you just read? If you could pick a single sentence out of the above statements that you need to believe the most, what would it be? Are you now able to see more clearly that error-filled thinking moves you away from the mind of God?

Self-Worth Without Self-Worship

What To Do

Putting it all together, try this experience. Whether at work or at home, keep an open notebook by your side for an entire day. Divide your paper into four columns. In the first column write down every worry and troubling thought that passes through your mind. (You will find that most troubling thoughts/feelings have to do with low self-esteem, including anger, envy, sadness, anxiety, fears, etc.) Later, analyze your thoughts by filling out the remaining three columns. In column two label your thoughts with the appropriate thinking errors. In the third column write down a good challenge question from the lists provided in this chapter that confronts your thinking error. Finally, in the fourth column write down an affirmative and healthy replacement thought.

Doing this exercise on paper will probably help you realize how many of the thinking errors trouble you day to day. This experience will also help get you into the habit of labeling your thoughts, criticizing them, and replacing them. By "renewing your mind" in this way, you will remove an important barrier to self-acceptance.

Chapter 6
THE
CURSE OF
PERFECTIONISM

A Most Common Curse

Jesus said, "For my yoke is easy and my burden is light" (Matthew 11:30). How many of us, though we know we are saved by grace and not by our works, have yolked ourselves with the awesome burden of perfectionism? How many of us live and work day to day with the internal pressure to do everything "just right?" How many of us live by a single standard in all we do, that is, the standard of perfection?

If you struggle in any way with low self-esteem, chances are you are victimized by the curse of perfectionism. Perfectionism is an extremely common condition. It is a kind of internal rigidity and tyranny. Perfectionism demands that you never do a project half-baked. It means shooting for an A or an A+ in whatever you do. Perfectionism paralyzes. It causes you to procrastinate or not act at all out of fear that you may prove yourself to be imperfect in some endeavor. Perfectionism drives you to having only one standard, immutable and ever-present.

Are you perfectionistic? Do you feel driven to always do your best in everything you attempt? Do you sometimes find yourself afraid to try something new out of fear that you won't be able to do it well? Do you seldom feel satisfied with your work? Do you ever get angry with yourself wishing you could just get the job done without worrying about every little detail and flaw? Do you drive yourself or other people around you crazy by worrying that it all comes out perfectly?

Perfectionism and low self-esteem are intricately linked. Each strengthens the other. If you are non-self-accepting, then it is likely that you emphasize performance and productivity as a measure of your worth. Thus, you are more likely to be perfectionistic. Yet, the stronger your tendency toward perfectionism, the less chance for self-acceptance. This is because demanding perfection of yourself sets you up for inevitable failure. This failure becomes translated into decreased self-esteem. So, without being aware, you can get caught up in the endless cycle of perfectionistic standards leading to inevitable dissatisfaction with yourself, which in turn compels you to more rigidly strive for perfectionism.

Perfectionism is no joke. It is exhausting and discouraging. It can infiltrate your life and impact virtually everything you do. Perfectionists can make the people that they live with crazy. I have seen much conflict and strained marriages when one partner is perfectionistic and the other has a more balanced and casual approach toward life. Perfectionism is indeed a curse. Fortunately, it is a curse from which you can be freed.

What The Bible Has To Say
The Scriptures tell us that God, Himself, is perfect. "As for God, his way is perfect" (2 Samuel 22:31). We know that our heavenly Father is perfect, but does His Word ask us to be perfect also? Surprisingly, it does. Consider the verse from Matthew 5:48, "Be perfect, therefore, as your heavenly Father is perfect." So what are we to do with this command that came

from Christ Himself? It must mean that our only standard *should* be perfectionism.

Before you feel justified in your own perfectionistic tendencies, let's take a closer look at this verse. "Be perfect" is stated in the progressive sense. That is, Christ is calling us to move closer to God and to strive to become more like Him as we go along. There is the establishment, through the model of Christ, of an ideal. But the Lord would not and does not ask of you that which is not humanly possible. The Word makes clear that perfection by your own efforts will never be possible as long as you live.

Even the apostle Paul admitted that he had not reached perfection, but instead emphasized his efforts at pressing on and moving *toward* the goal (Philippians 3:12). What Paul tried to give us was a description of a process that is unfinished on earth and a striving that is unattainable without faith and futile without Christ. The perfection in you as demanded from God occurs only through Christ. Through faith you are indeed presented perfectly in Christ (Colossians 1:28), and further, you are "made perfect forever" by Christ (Hebrews 10:14). That is why Jesus is called "the author and perfecter of our faith" (Hebrews 12:2). You will never be able to present yourself as perfect before God by your own efforts no matter how hard you try. Romans 3:28 tells us, "For we maintain that a man is justified by faith apart from observing the law." If it were in any way possible for you to be perfect, then the need for God to send His only Son has been eliminated. Consider Hebrews 7:11 which says, "If perfection could have been obtained...why was there still need for another priest to come . . . ?"

Reflect upon this amazing thought for a moment: if you are a believer in the Lord Jesus Christ, you have already been made perfect in the eyes of God.

Be aware that the perfectionism that takes up much of your time and energy has little to do with being perfect in a spiritual sense in any case. Most of your perfectionism has to do with your job, your projects, and the impression that you are trying to make on others. The kind of unending perfectionism that plagues most of us ultimately has little to do with holiness. In fact, one way to look at it is that in your own strivings to be perfect, you not only usurp God's authority, but you also separate yourself from your dependence on Him. "It is God who arms me with strength and makes my way perfect" (Psalm 18:32).

Signs and Symptoms
Perfectionism, like so many other ways that you think about and treat yourself, has likely been with you for so long that you are hardly aware that it is there. Let's look at some typical signs and symptoms of perfectionism to see which ones sound familiar to you. Perfectionism is a complex, multifaceted feature which will display itself in some of the following manifestations:

1. **Excessive need for control**. This is a strong need to control yourself, your emotions and actions, and the people and events around you. Perfectionists seem to have a strong need to be always on top of things. They become anxious when they sense that things are getting beyond them or out of their control.

2. **Rigidity**. Perfectionists tend to have a strict and set way of doing things. They

also tend to view the world in a way that leaves little room for deviation and flexibility. Perfectionists tend to be restricted in the way they think, function, and even in the feelings they allow themselves.

3. **Problems with ambiguity.** This has to do with discomfort with concepts that are vague and not easily understood in terms of well-defined categories. To be asked a question that can be interpreted in more than one way illustrates ambiguity since there is a lack of surety about what the questioner actually means. This can be troubling to the precision-minded perfectionist.

4. **Worrisomeness.** Perfectionists often spend much time in idle worry. Worry can be viewed as a way of attempting to control situations. Perfectionists often feel that if they worry about something then that represents a way of staying on top of it.

5. **Indecisiveness.** Perfectionists are indecisive out of fear of making the "wrong" decision. Perfectionists often spend a lot of time "sitting on the fence." Indecisiveness can be quite uncomfortable and at times even costly.

6. **Dissatisfaction.** Perfectionists seldom feel fully satisfied with a job well done. They tend to view things with a highly critical eye, especially their own work.

111

They are quite adept at picking out flaws and second-guessing how things should have or could have been done differently.

7.   **Overly serious.** People who are perfectionistic often have an overly sober outlook on life. After all, if there is no room for imperfection, how could you feel casual about moving through life? Perfectionists sometimes hear comments from their friends like, "Lighten up."

8.   **Fear of taking risks.** Perfectionists are fearful of taking chances because things may not work out "right." Perfectionists can become stilted and stagnant in their lives by never taking appropriate risks.

9.   **Pleasureless drive through life.** Perfectionists are apt victims of the pleasureless drive. They are adept at defeating any chance of experiencing the simple joy of just being. Striving for achievement can become a preoccupation when the only standard is perfection.

10.   **Damaged relationships.** People who are perfectionistic are often very demanding of those around them. Perfectionism means inflexibility with others as well as yourself.

11.   **Poor tolerance for interference with plans and methods.** Perfectionists have standard and routine ways of doing

things and become upset when people interfere with the "right way."

12. **Difficulty seeking pleasure for pleasure's sake.** Perfectionists often feel that they have to be productive at all times. After all, it is time-consuming to be perfect. Perfectionists often saddle themselves with a long list of tasks that must be completed before they will allow themselves to relax.

13. **Inability to "let go."** This is the inability to "let the chips fall where they may," "let God," and to cease attempting to be on top of everything. Perfectionists try to have all their bases covered at all times and are fearful of letting events run their natural course.

14. **Excessive planning.** Perfectionists usually work very hard at having everything laid out in advance. It is just easier to be perfect that way.

15. **Excessive concerns for what others think.** Perfectionists have a need to be seen as perfect by others. Perfectionists have a way of assuming that the people around them have the same excessive demands that the perfectionist places on himself or herself.

16. **Decreased tolerance for mistakes.** Perfectionists, very often, have *no* tolerance for mistakes. They tend to berate themselves for every blunder and

error. Perfectionists often are also intolerant of mistakes in others.

17. **Excessive concern with details.** Perfectionists are usually detail-oriented, even to the point that it interferes with their getting the job done. A good perfectionist can become so stymied by a minor detail that he or she might be unable to move forward to complete a task.

18. **Black-and-white thinking.** Perfectionists tend to view themselves and their tasks in either-or, all-or-none terms. They tend to categorize their efforts as being, for example, perfect or disastrous, great or awful. They have trouble viewing things in terms of shades of gray.

19. **Excessive prudence and discipline.** Perfectionists tend to overvalue ideals such as loyalty, prudence, and self-discipline. They tend to hold onto and demand of themselves unwavering ideals having to do with what is proper and acceptable.

Do any of the above nineteen indicators sound familiar to you? How many of them describe the way that you have approached your life? Do not be surprised if many of them apply. Unless you are completely self-accepting, the curse of perfectionism is a likely companion.

Self-Worth Without Self-Worship

Where Perfectionism Is Found

People who are not self-accepting tend to be perfection-istic across a wide variety of situations. Perfectionism helps to dictate not only performance and behaviors, but also thoughts and feelings. People often feel that they need to be perfect in the roles that they play, for example, as a parent, spouse, or homemaker. Perfec-tionism is especially apparent on the job. Many individuals are driven to be perfectly competent at all times in their career. Some individuals strive to show perfection in altruism and pleasing others. Perfection may also become the standard in the area of morality. Still, others attempt to mistake-proof their lives and strive for a life free from failure.

Where are your areas of perfectionism? Perhaps you believe you should show perfect judgment in all decisions that you make and in your problem-solving abilities. Maybe you think you need to be perfectly self-sufficient, never leaning on or becoming dependent upon others. Perhaps you try to be perfectly "normal," displaying an evenness and stability in all of your emotions. Do you saddle yourself with the belief that you must always do your best? Are you aware that incessantly demanding of yourself that you do your absolute best is a form of perfectionism?

Perfectionism can become a constant companion. It can interfere with what you allow yourself to feel, do, or think. Where does perfectionism most show itself in your life?

Counting The Costs

Being perfect is an exceedingly demanding way to live. It is helpful to recognize that perfectionism comes from within. It is not demanded of you by God and it usually is not expected by the people around you. People usually demand perfection of themselves. Perfectionism can exact a tremendous toll on your life.

To begin with, perfectionism is exhausting. Having to do everything just so and being on top of things at all times, can produce a bitter weariness. On the job, burnout is more likely because perfectionism contributes to the pleasureless drive. While working, perfectionists often become lost in detail, using up ninety percent of their energy completing only ten percent of the whole task. Perfectionism is a main culprit in procrastination. You are more likely to put things off and not complete projects if you make yourself wait until you are sure you can do them perfectly. At its extreme, this procrastination can lead to absolute paralysis. The fear of imperfect performance may cause you to freeze up completely. Many a first step have not taken place, many an adventure not undertaken, and many a job have been left uninitiated by the one who fears all imperfection.

There can be emotional costs to you if you are perfectionistic. There may be a tendency to give up easily at the first sign that things aren't going exactly as planned and a sense of resignation can result. Worries and fears are also more prominent when you are perfectionistic especially in the areas of performance or evaluation. Indecisiveness often accompanies perfectionism and this too can be an exhausting and costly burden. Generally, perfectionists tend to focus on the past (reviewing mistakes) and the future (anticipating future failure) and have difficulty just living in and enjoying the present moment.

Another arena of cost to you if you are perfectionistic, is in your relationships. As previously mentioned, perfectionists can be difficult to live with. Their self-demanding style often becomes translated into a demandingness or a faultfinding habit in their attitudes toward others. Perfectionists often place performance in a higher position than good relationships. As a result, perfectionists may be overly pleasing and even timid out of fear of saying or doing the wrong thing and being met with disapproval.

Finally, perfectionism is the opposite of peace. It damages your self-esteem because it makes your self-acceptance dependent upon your ability to be perfect, an obviously unreachable goal. Perfectionism hurts your walk with the Lord because you are failing to relax in your perfection through Christ and instead are seeking perfection through your own works.

What To Do
If you find yourself in any way being perfectionistic
here are some things to try.

1. First of all, make a decision to begin to
    let go of your perfectionism. In fact,
    take on an attitude of reveling in your
    imperfection. See your human imperfec-
    tion as representing uniqueness. Learn
    to laugh at yourself, your foibles, your
    flaws, your failures.

2. Review the list of signs and symptoms
    of perfectionism and try some behaviors
    that are just the opposite. For example,
    let's say that one of the manifestations
    from your perfectionism is an excessive
    need to control. Out of this problem
    you find yourself frustrated each evening
    trying to get everyone home in time for
    dinner, which you always have ready
    promptly at six. Perhaps you are unhap-
    py with yourself for nagging and badger-
    ing as you attempt to round up the
    family each evening. A good opposite
    behavior to try would be to prepare
    dinner, sit down by yourself at six
    o'clock and begin to eat. You might
    learn that in your attempt to be less
    controlling, and thus less perfectionistic,
    your family members become more self-
    initiating and show up for dinner after
    all.

3. Practice messing up on purpose. Take
    some unessential task and execute it
    poorly. There can be a sense of liberty

in purposefully building in mistakes because being imperfect on purpose desensitizes you to imperfection. Remember, anything worth doing is worth doing wrong.

4. Engage in some pleasurable activities with which your perfectionism has previously interfered. For example, if you never go on family outings on Saturdays until the house is clean, the cars are washed, and all the errands are run, try something new next weekend. Get up early, pack the family in the car and just go. Stop letting the excessive demands of perfectionism rob you of fun.

5. Develop some new attitudes. As you begin projects, shoot for a B instead of an A. Remind yourself that letting go of perfectionism will not turn you into a lazy, obnoxious slob. Challenge yourself to be less than perfect. Ask yourself to be flexible and balanced in how hard you work on the job and at home.

6. Replace your demand that you always do your "best" with the word "effortful." Asking yourself to be effortful rather than always having to do your absolute best gives you a flexible range of effort rather than a singular, rigid standard. Be effortful, don't be perfect.

7. Count the costs. Review the various arenas of probable cost from your per-

fectionism. Become aware of the peaceful, abundant life of which your perfectionism is a thief. Note especially how perfectionism interferes with your need for greater self-acceptance and a closer walk with the Lord.

8.   Focus on the phrase "letting go." Letting go means different things to different people. If you were to approach life with more an attitude of letting go, letting God, and letting things run their natural course, what would you do differently?

9.   Try something that you have been afraid of trying because of the paralysis of perfectionism. Go ahead and take that class even though you may flunk it. Engage someone in conversation even though you might not always know the exact and correct thing to say. Apply for that new job even though you may not be the perfect candidate.

10.   Reflect upon and recognize the absurdity of perfectionism. Be aware that nothing that you have ever done nor will ever do can be done perfectly. What is more, there is not much in life that *needs* to be done perfectly. Even if you could do something perfectly, it would be very difficult to tell when a job is perfectly done.

11.   You set the standards, you can change them. In your day-to-day work, and

your relationships, and in the impressions that you make on others, God does not ask of you to be perfect. He would never ask something of you that you are not capable of doing. Why do you do that to yourself? Don't be *perfect*, just be *perfected*.

12. Take time to reflect on God's provision by which you are perfected.

Chapter 7
THE ORIGIN
OF YOUR
SELF-ESTEEM

Barbara grew up with an alcoholic father. Until she was old enough to spend much time in friends' homes, she thought all dads got drunk most nights. For Barbara, helping her mother drag her stuporous father up the steps for bed each night was simply a part of the normal daily routine.

Barbara was afraid of her father, especially when he took off his shoes and socks. When he did this, with drink in hand, he was becoming drunk enough for the rages to start. Slammed doors, smashed dishes, threats, and screaming insults terrified her. She spent many a night alone in her room with her fingers in her ears, singing quietly to herself to drown out the bellowing fights between her father and mother. Barbara learned to steer clear of her father when he was becoming drunk because she too had been the target of his drunken rages. When the shoes and socks came off, she knew it was time to hide.

Being the oldest, Barbara had an extra burden. She felt that she was the only one who could take care of her little brother and she did her best to protect him from their father. Barbara's mother was emotionally neglectful of her two children due to her own preoccupation with her husband's alcoholic and abusive nature. Except for the role that she played as a little mother,

Barbara grew up feeling that she did not count for much. Little attention was paid by her parents to her schooling and other activities. Because of the constant turmoil in the house, no one was there to quell her fears or tell her that she was loved. Barbara tried to be the perfect little girl. "Perhaps Dad won't drink tonight", she reasoned, "if I'm really a good girl. Maybe if Mom sees how good my grades are, she will pay attention to me."

Because her father often railed against her directly, Barbara sometimes felt that it was her fault that her father was drinking. When he was not yelling at her, he was ignoring her. She felt invisible yet full of shame. She was embarrassed to bring friends home lest they see the disarray that characterized her home life. Except for her ability to play the role of a mother to her little brother, Barbara grew up feeling entirely worthless. Even after moving out of her home and getting married, Barbara could not seem to shake the ever-present sense that she was a bad person.

A Look At Your Childhood
You can imagine the kinds of messages that Barbara received as a child about herself and her value as a person. Barbara grew up believing that her needs did not matter and therefore, she, herself, was not important. It is likely that she came away with the erroneous belief that she somehow deserved her father's tirades and was perhaps to blame for some of his drunken episodes. Furthermore, Barbara was probably left with the sense that her entire value was contingent upon her ability to be a caretaker for others, such as she had been for her little brother.

But what about you? What kinds of messages did you receive as a child? What happened to you while you

124

were growing up and what aspects of your relationship with your parents affected your self-esteem? Did you grow up believing that you were not okay just as you were?

Jesus had a special place in his heart for preciousness of children. In the 10th chapter of the Gospel of Mark, Jesus demanded that the children be brought to Him, "Let the little children come to me, and do not hinder them, for the kingdom of God belongs to such as these." Then later the Word tells us, ". . . he took the children in his arms, put his hands on them and blessed them" (vv. 14 and 16). Surely Jesus knew of the special needs and vulnerabilities of children. He knew how suggestible and sensitive they were. You were no less innocent and vulnerable as a young child. The way you were treated and the messages you received about yourself as a child is why your self-esteem is where it is today.

Though it isn't always a pleasant thing to do, it can be helpful for you to take a look back at your formative years in order to help determine the development of your self-esteem. Your tendency toward self-acceptance or the lack of therein probably began back before you can remember. But even though specific events may not be easily brought to recollection, you can look at the general atmosphere of your childhood and make guesses as to how this helped form your degree of self-esteem.

God calls us to know and practice the truth (Psalm 51:6). Taking an open and frank look at your childhood is a way of seeking truth. Looking honestly at the way you were raised may not always be flattering to your caretakers. However, the goal here is to get a better idea of why you feel the way you do about yourself, not to pass judgment on your parents for whatever they may or may not have done correctly. In fact, later in this chapter is an exhortation for you to focus on forgiving your parents if, indeed, that is in order for you.

What Children Perceive
Before looking at some specifics from your childhood, let's take a look at some of the ways that children generally perceive their world. First of all, children believe what they are told. If they are told that they are bad, then that is exactly where the core of their self-esteem will be. Second, children tend to blame themselves rather than their parents. Young children do not have the capacity to critically analyze a situation and determine, for example, that mother is simply in a bad mood. Rather, the child is likely to interpret mom's irritability as being a negative reflection on the child. Third, children generally believe they have more power to control the events around them than they really do. For example, a child may blame himself or herself for the parents' divorce as if he or she could have done something to stop it. Fourth, unless you were told and made to believe without question that you were good enough just being you, you tended to believe the opposite. Unless children are blessed with the sense that they are loved unconditionally by their parents, they will either feel unlovable or that any love they receive is contingent upon their good behavior. Finally, during the development of self-esteem, certain emotional reactions or gut feelings were set firmly into place. Though the names and faces have changed, your gut reactions toward yourself today are identical to the way you felt as a child, even though you may not remember the specific events that caused those feelings.

Self-Worth Without Self-Worship

Seeking the truth about the origin of your self-esteem can be valuable but painful. For many of us, looking back is unpleasant. In reality, few of us have had a truly idyllic childhood with all of the images of child-like abandon, carefree days of wonderment, and endless fun. For many, what will be recalled was a tense time of trial and error, vulnerability, fears, and stress. Some may have had a childhood filled with early responsibilities, worries, and perceived failures. For still others, abuse, abandonment, neglect, and loneliness were the rule. So why do it? Why dredge up old history which may make you feel sad and angry? First, understanding is knowledge, and knowledge is power. With this power you can change. Your self-esteem started when you were very young. Looking at the nature of your origins of your self-esteem can shed light on the nature of your self-esteem now. Seeing the fallacy of what you believed then can give you impetus to reject current false beliefs since most of your beliefs have roots in early childhood.

The Subtle Message
Because you, like most children, were probably exqui-sitely sensitive to your parents' attitudes toward you, it is important to look at some common subtle yet negative messages to which children are often subject-ed. We have already noted that simply never being told that you were in any way good enough probably caused you to assume just the opposite. You do not need a history of being overtly belittled to have grown up believing that you were inferior. Consider the child who brings home a report card with mostly A's and one B. The parent, while recognizing overall that the grades are good, is quick to ask, "Why is there a B?" Other subtle messages of not being worthwhile may come about when a parent does not take time to ade-quately respond to appropriate questions from the child.

"Never mind, you wouldn't understand." Children sometimes find themselves being made to feel guilty because of natural curiosity leading to questions about sex, family problems, etc. Like many children, perhaps you were also carefully taught that you were not to "toot your own horn." The subtlety here is that you learn that it is okay to be critical of yourself but not to recognize strengths and areas of achievement. Other subtle messages include statements such as "good children don't do that," with the implication being that your value or goodness is based only on your behaviors. Additionally, subtle but self-esteem-damaging messages are often received by children through acts of omission by their parents. Some children are never complimented, touched in loving ways, or simply told, "I love you."

How comfortable were your parents with your open displays of emotion? Were you unintentionally taught to "stuff" your feelings? Common comments include, "If you are going to cry, then go to your room," or "Stop crying or I'll give you something to cry about." Perhaps you were told that you were "too big" to be afraid of the dark. The hidden messages here are that expressing and perhaps even feeling sadness, fear, and anger, makes you a bad person. You may have learned to deny what you really felt and consequently who you were as a child. This can leave you with an abiding sense that your very essence is not okay since what comes natural to you must be shut down.

Another subtle message that many children receive that can be damaging to self-esteem occurs when the child is treated as a little adult. This can come about when the child is given too many adult-like responsibilities or children who are treated as companions and confidants by a parent. Barbara, whose story opened this chapter,

128

is just such an example. The subtle message is that being a child is not okay and doing childlike things makes one "bad." Did you ever feel a sense that you needed to hurry to be grown up and force yourself to act in grown up ways before you were developmentally ready? Children need to be allowed to be just children and to be valued as such. Part of what it means to be a child is to be emotional, expressive, needy, self-centered, and mistake-prone. Children may cause embarrassment to their parents. They can be boring, trite, and rambling in their speech. In spite of these childlike behaviors, they need to be given positive regard and special attention. It is probably best to think of child-rearing in this way: children should not be treated like adults, but should be accorded the same respect as adults. Were you raised with these attitudes?

Finally, if you were ignored in any way as a child, you received a covert yet negative message of your worth as a human being. Children simply want to be acknowledged and to feel that they are "good enough" as a child. Think of the child who runs excitedly home from school to present a completed masterpiece of art work to mom, only to be met with, "Wipe your feet and put your things away," while having the art work essentially ignored. Usually if a child's achievements in school or in extracurricular activities are ignored or minimized, the child will attempt to do better even to the point of perfectionism in order to gain approval and recognition. This may set up a pattern of perfectionistic rigidity, even into adulthood, and a permanent sense of never quite being "good enough." If you were not met with at least occasional recognition and compliments for achievements, then it is likely you assumed that somehow you were falling short and were defective. You do not need to have been belittled in order to draw the conclusion that you were not a worthwhile individual. Even a neutral response by your parents could have evoked the conclusion from you that you were not okay.

Childhood Abuse

Some parental messages that children receive are not so subtle. Certain messages that can absolutely destroy a child's self-esteem are viscous enough to be considered emotional abuse. Constant name-calling, excessive screaming, or being ignored for long periods of time are examples of emotional abuse. Emotional abuse can come in a variety of packages. Sometimes a child is placed in a position of being a pawn and a go-between for two parents at odds with one another. Children can be emotionally tortured with extreme threats such as being killed for misbehaviors and/or being threatened with religious condemnation. Low self-esteem also results from comments such as, "I wish you were never born."

Another form of emotional abuse is when you are forced to view significant conflict between mother and father or watch one parent abuse the other. Emotional abuse can also take the form of severe inconsistencies in the messages from your parents that you may have received as a child. This may happen if one of your behaviors seems to be funny and okay one day, but is severely punished the next. In this way, you may have been left guessing as to what was acceptable behavior and what your parents' moods might be at any given time. Some have coined the term "rageaholism" to designate someone who regularly explodes into frightening and unpredictable tirades. If your parent was a "rageaholic," this may have left you feeling frightened, belittled, and somehow to blame for the angry outbursts.

Self-Worth Without Self-Worship

Emotional abuse can happen quickly and in almost any setting. I once stood in a grocery line behind an obviously exasperated mother who called her five-year-old son a term representing human excrement. I wondered to myself how that child could ever grow up with any semblance of self-acceptance in the midst of being referred to in such vulgar terms. Another child, a three-year-old, was required to enter speech therapy because he was having trouble learning to talk. His father, perhaps out of personal embarrassment, referred to his son as "a fool." Threats of being disowned by the parent is another form of emotional abuse. One female patient of mine was repeatedly driven past a local orphanage by her mother under threats of being sent there if her behavior did not improve. My patient recalls the sight of this dreary institution being terrifying to her. It was no wonder that this individual in her adult years felt that she was no good.

Other forms of emotional abuse are perhaps not as obvious, but can be equally devastating. For example, did your parents try to control your behaviors by using excessive guilt and fear or physical intimidation? Were you ever criticized in front of others or was any other form of embarrassment used to discipline you?

Were you emotionally abused in any way? How did this treatment affect your self-esteem?

Physical abuse can be equally damaging to a child's self-esteem. Physical abuse ranges from mild to severe, including systematic and ritualistic torture. Some of the damage of physical abuse occurs because it often takes place in combination with emotional abuse. Being hit by someone is, at the very least, humiliating. If you were physically abused, you almost definitely concluded that you were somehow "bad."

Remember, children tend to see themselves as the center of blame before blaming the parent. This is even true in children who were severely abused. Was physical abuse a part of your childhood years?

Another form of abuse that can be both physical and emotional is called neglect. I had a patient who was punished by her father by being sent to bed hungry and forced to sleep in a room where the father refused to turn on the heat. Children who are neglected learn that their needs do not matter and, therefore, that they do not matter.

Finally, is the issue of sexual abuse. Sexual abuse occurs when a child is used in any fashion for the sexual pleasure of an adult. This includes fondling, intercourse, and other obviously sexual acts, but may also take subtler forms such as leering, intrusive sexual questions and comments, and inappropriate nudity around the house. This type of abuse is shockingly common with estimates of one-quarter or more of all girls and one-tenth of all boys being victims. If you are one of these many victims, then you are certainly not alone.

If you were sexually abused, your self-esteem is likely to be nil. Self-blame, or the victim blaming the victim, is almost universal with this kind of abuse. Even very young children seem to instinctively know that there is something "bad" about sexual contact between themselves and an adult. Self-blame is compounded because the child may actually like certain elements of the sexual abuse such as closeness and attention from the abuser. Sex abuse victims also tend to make the assumption that they should have somehow stopped the abuse. If you were sexually abused, it is likely that you have tended to forget how dependent, vulnerable, and otherwise limited you were in your ability to escape your abusive situation.

Were you abused in any way as a child, emotionally, physically, or sexually? If so, what do you think were your interpretations of such abuse related to your own sense of self-regard? (If you were severely abused as a child in any way and especially if you were sexually abused, it is recommended that you consider spending some time with a good professional therapist. Sometimes, professional counselling is the only way to adequately work through some types of abuse in order to more fully get on with your life.)

The Dysfunctional Family

Children who grew up in dysfunctional families are usually saddled with a lifetime of struggling with their own self-acceptance. A dysfunctional family is one in which there is significant chaos, unpredictability, and emotional illness. Parental needs take consistent priority over the needs of the children. If you grew up in a family that was secretive, conflictful, or one in which instability and unpredictability were the rule, then your family can be considered to have been dysfunctional. Usually there is an unspoken conspiracy of silently pretending that there are no problems. The emotional needs of one or both parents are often so extreme that the struggle to manage them causes neglect of the emotional and physical demands of the children. If you grew up in a dysfunctional family, you may have begun to see emotional pain as normal and ultimately concluded that you perhaps did not deserve any better.

Barbara's story is a common example of a dysfunctional family. Her father was an alcoholic and the result was a parent who was moody, inconsistent, and unpredictable. Barbara grew up feeling unimportant because she could not depend on her father. This not-being-taken-care-of feeling was exacerbated by the fact that her mother was distracted by her husband's alcoholism and may have been attempting to control his drinking behavior to the neglect of her own children. We call the mother's problem "co-dependency." What this meant for Barbara was that both of her parents were emotionally unstable and inconsistently available for her wants and needs. If this describes your family, you may have blamed yourself for your parents' preoccupations and the constant emotional upheaval. You may also have felt confused and, therefore "stupid" by your inability to predict and control your parents' behaviors and moods. You may have even tried to control family events but failed on a regular basis. You may have learned to see yourself as a failure. Additionally, you may have not been allowed to be simply a child but rather felt a need to become a little adult in order to try to take care of family problems.

Dysfunction in a family may also manifest itself in the wake of divorce. The impact of the parents' divorce on self-esteem depends on the age of the child and how the child is cared for during and after the divorce. It is not unusual for the child to feel blameworthy for the parents' divorce. Young children, especially, need to be assured that they could have neither caused nor prevented their parents' divorce. They need to be told that the divorce had nothing to do with their being "bad boys" or "bad girls." The problem is, however, that in the aftermath of divorce with both parents being emotionally upset, the child's needs are often neglected.

If divorce was a part of your growing up experience, you may also have been hurt by being burdened by one or both of the parents using you as an emotional crutch. This can be especially harmful if one parent spoke negatively about the other parent to you or used you to somehow manipulate the ex-spouse. Self-esteem is endangered here because you may have felt guilty for complicity with one parent against the other. You may also have tried to bring the parents back together only to be doomed to failure. Feeling unloved and abandoned may also have been a theme for you as the logistics of shared parenting became an issue. Finally, the remarriage of one or both parents may have left you feeling abandoned, neglected, or otherwise unimportant and unloved.

If you grew up in a family that displayed significant dysfunction then it is highly likely that you will struggle with becoming more self-accepting. You may have learned to use excessive control of others, chemical dependency, and other destructive and unhealthy ways of functioning because healthy modes of coping were not modeled for you. You may also use avoidance of problems as a method of coping. Adults from dysfunctional families often have a confused sense of what love and caring is, and you may be left unable to have your emotional needs met and to feel good about meeting the needs of others. Do any of the above characteristics sound like you? How different would things be in your life if you reached a place of true self-acceptance?

Basic Messages
In our attempt to gain some perspective on the origins of your self-esteem, we have covered the things that can go wrong in the way that your parents related to you. We have looked at some of the subtle messages that you may have received as a child as well as the self-esteem implications in being raised by parents who were abusive or otherwise dysfunctional. The crucial scars that last a lifetime are those beliefs about yourself that interfere with self-acceptance that grew out of your

135

interpretation of parental messages. In other words, the most far-reaching and long-term effects from the nature of your childhood come from how your childhood led you to feel about your own value.

Most negative parental messages can be summarized in just a handful of basic ideas. See if any of these core messages sound familiar to you. You may have come away believing that your parents said to you:

1. *"I don't care."*
2. *"You are a bad person."*
3. *"You are in the way, a bother, a hardship."*
4. *"Be a little adult."*
5. *"Don't express yourself, especially your emotions and opinions."*
6. *"You are never quite good enough."*

What do you imagine would be the impact on your self-esteem from each of these basic six messages? With which of these messages were you indoctrinated as a child because of the way your parents related to you?

A Word About Forgiveness
Learning to become more self-accepting is actually a search for truth. That search for truth includes an honest appraisal of the way that you were raised. If, in looking back, you realize that the way you were raised was far from ideal (and this is usually the case), you may find yourself experiencing anger at your primary caretakers. Feeling angry has its place and should not be a source of guilt for you. However, it is not good to remain "stuck" in a place of anger. Long-term anger becomes bitterness and bitterness helps no one. Look

frankly and openly at your childhood, allowing your anger to emerge as appropriate; but, without waiting too long, come to a decision to forgive.

You need to forgive your parents primarily because doing so is an act of obedience. Christ Himself called us to forgive anyone that we hold anything against (Mark 11:25). As in all other commands from God, the Lord knows that to be obedient in this way is the best thing for you in the long run and the best thing for the relationship with your parents. Keep in mind that your parents were imperfect beings who struggled with their own self-esteem problems. There is no way that your parents could have anticipated and met all of your needs as a child. Good parenting is the most difficult job there is and, because it is more an art than a science, will never be done to everyone's satisfaction. It is also important to keep in mind that some of the negative messages you may have received as a child had to do with your *misinterpretations* of aspects of your relationship with your parents. Finally, as you are about to see, not all of the battering that your self-esteem took as a child came from your parents.

Forgive your parents. Make an honest appraisal about the way you were raised. Allow yourself only a season of anger, and then make the decision to forgive, fully and with a prayerful heart.

Lest we become needlessly pessimistic about the nature of your childhood, let us take a moment to consider some positive parental features. In what ways did your parents actually help to increase your self-esteem? Did they help you feel good about your accomplishments and successes? Did they give adequate attention to you and your activities? In what ways were you allowed to be just a child? Did you, in anyway, feel significant and important in your family? In what way did your parents provide a haven for you and safety against the wiles of the outside world? In what ways were you lovingly touched and told that you were loved? Can you remember special times together? Was either parent considerate and respectful of you?

Other Childhood Circumstances
Let us take a look at other aspects of childhood that may have influenced the development of your self-esteem.

Other Adults. Though your parents were the most important determiners of the nature of your self-esteem, there may have been other influential adults from your past, having both positive and negative impact on you. For example, most of us have had good and bad teachers. Perhaps you were influenced by members of the clergy or other fellow worshipers. Consider the parents of your childhood friends, your neighbors, and any other adults who may have played a role in the development of your sense of self. Extended family members should also be considered here, including aunts, uncles, and grandparents. Think about the expectations these adults had for you. Were any of these adults abusive? How did these people make you feel about yourself when you were little?

Children's Cruelty to Children. Important to your experience as a child were your peer relationships. What were your relationships with your friends like? How were you treated by other children in the neighborhood or at school? Children can be amazingly cruel to other children, even to their best friends. They often communicate in hurtful ways by saying, "Go away, we don't want to play with you." They are often physically aggressive, showing low frustration tolerance and taking their anger out on their peers. Children will often side with their peers against others and frequently gang up on a single individual. How did the actions of the kids around you impact your self-esteem?

Critical Events. Critical events are certain key moments that stand out in your childhood. These critical moments are events or series of events that seem to stick with you. We are talking about negative occurrences in your childhood that you know without question were traumatic or otherwise impactful. Critical events can include things such as a school failure, death of a close relative, a particularly harsh punishment, or any other emotionally charged event. As you reflect on critical events from your childhood, be sure to include any happenings that may have been rather minor except that they were repeated. For example, being taunted by bullies after school one day may not have undermined your self-esteem as a child. However, if the bullying incidents became a daily affair over a protracted period, definite psychological damage may have been done. Your critical childhood events may have taken place anywhere, but most likely occurred in your home. Other places to consider include schools, the playground, your neighborhood, or church. These events may have involved family members including siblings, your peers, or may have taken place while you were alone.

Special Circumstances. There may have been particular life circumstances in your childhood that gave rise to certain negative feelings about yourself. For example, perhaps you were raised in a very large family. While this may have certain advantages, taking care of a large family may have left your parents tired, distracted, and unavailable. Perhaps privacy was lacking as well as financial resources. One important special life circumstance affecting childhood is that of growing up in poverty. Poor children often feel inferior by virtue of not having what others have. Children who are poor are often the victim of prejudices and certainly experience more than their share of cruelty from their peers. Growing up as a racial or an ethnic minority can also have great impact on a child's self-esteem. Minority children must battle with feeling misunderstood, isolated, and inferior. They are often the victims of overt prejudices and even hatred. Other special circumstances that may have affected your self-esteem include living in a family that frequently relocated, living in a rural and isolated area, being raised in a one parent family, or growing up physically "different" such as being overweight or having a physical handicap.

Birth Order. Another circumstance that can be an important determiner in the development of your self-esteem is your birth order. Were you the oldest child? The youngest? Or were you an only child? How did your position among your brothers and sisters affect your self-esteem? First-born children may suffer from a lack of self-acceptance because of having experienced more demands on them from their parents. A middle child may struggle with self-esteem from having to compete with an older sibling. Other special pressures may be present for the youngest child or for an only child. Which position in the order of birth do you think is the most favorable for healthy emotional development?

The Pervasive Sexism. All of us have been affected by the pervasive sexism in our culture. Sexist ideas and attitudes are disseminated through families and society in general. Sexism is passed along by both men and women. It damages the self-esteem of both genders.   Sexism teaches children that they have limitations or must fill particular roles based solely on gender. For example, children learn that girls become homemakers, but boys do not. What impressions about the nature of the roles of men and women did you get as a child? What was your father's attitude toward women? How did your mother view men? What sexist attitudes did you adopt for yourself?

What To Do

1.   Become aware. Though it may be difficult, reflect back on your childhood and see what you can figure out regarding the origins of your self-esteem. Consider the way your parents treated you, any critical events, your special circumstances, and any other aspects from your early years that influenced the way you valued and evaluated yourself. See if you can remember how you felt about yourself as a child and how that influences your sense of self-regard today.

2.   Forgive your parents for any mistakes that they might have made and forgive anyone else who may have negatively influenced you as a child. Make forgiveness your choice but let the love of God through the power of the Holy Spirit in your life work through you to bring forgiveness to completion.

3.   Go back through this chapter and answer on paper the questions that were presented there. For example, write out the messages that you received, the nature of dysfunction and abuse in your family, any critical events, etc. Develop a word portrait of your childhood with special emphasis on how the circumstances of your early years influenced your self-esteem.

4.   Summarize the messages and the lies you took from childhood. As a naive

and suggestible child, you probably believed things about yourself that were not true. Many of these lies are now perpetuated in your adult self-evaluations. Identify and articulate what some of these false messages were.

5. Write a letter to the "little you." Picture yourself at age seven or eight and imagine what you most needed to hear. Write the things that would have most helped you to accept and like yourself as a child. Tell the child what you would like to do for him or her. Give this exercise some thought and write a nice, full letter. Begin to develop a heart for the child you were. This will make it easier for you to develop self-acceptance as an adult.

6. Pray for release and separation from the negative aspects of your childhood. Ask that any scars be uncovered and to be shown the way to healing if needed.

Chapter 8
THE PROBLEM EMOTIONS

Three Problem Emotions
Depression, anxiety, and anger are three packages of emotions that probably all of us have experienced at one time or another. At issue here is the interplay between these three emotional conditions and self-esteem. As we will see, people who are lacking in self-acceptance are more susceptible to feeling depressed, anxious, or angry. It is more difficult, for example to suffer from the blues when you are experiencing true peace with who you are. It's less likely that you will be nervous or anxious about your future if you are confident about your ability to manage any difficulties that come your way. Additionally, you will have fewer problems with anger as you become less sensitive of what others think of you and your "ego" is less fragile.

The basic idea is that low self-esteem fosters a susceptibility to suffering from depression, anxiety, and inappropriate anger. In addition to experiencing more of these negative emotions when self-esteem is low, it is also common to thrash and trash yourself because you are having these experiences. In other words, low self-esteem contributes to emotional disturbance. Emotional upheaval, in turn, can short circuit one's efforts toward self-acceptance. However, addressing any self-esteem problems and becoming more self-accepting can provide an elixir in the battle against the problem emotions.

Depression

Depression is the most common thing I see in my psychotherapy practice. Depression has been called the common cold of mental health. With symptoms ranging from mild to severe, people with depression sometimes suffer for years or even decades before seeking help. If not treated, depression can be a fatal condition as the desire to commit suicide is often part of the symptom package. Depression is found in about twice as many women as men.

Depression can be paralyzing and debilitating. It can sap the meaning out of your life and send you to bed for weeks at a time. Depression can make everything seem like a monumental chore and it can undermine even strong relationships. People have lost their jobs and marriages have fallen apart because of depression.

The problem is that depression is bad enough without the guilt and pressure some people heap on their own heads simply because they are experiencing depression. As if the depressed feelings were not enough, people with low self-esteem call themselves names such as "crazy" or "lazy" when they are depressed and unfairly blame themselves for their blues. Low self-esteem compounds depression. Self-acceptance, however, can be a way out.

Paula has been depressed for many years. In fact, when she looks back, she believes she may have been depressed even as a little girl. Lately, Paula's depression has been getting much worse. The world looks stark and colorless to her. She has withdrawn from her friends, believing that they would not want to be around her while she is feeling so out of sorts. She feels sad most of the time and cries over almost anything. She feels tired a lot and only through great effort does she drag herself through the work day. She feels vaguely sick to her stomach and has been losing weight. Nothing seems appetizing to her and when she comes home from work she would just as soon go to bed than fix supper. Paula has never felt like such a loser and she wonders why she can't be simply happy with the good things she has. She battles with trying to keep away from thoughts of suicide.

Have you ever experienced some of the symptoms Paula has? Have you ever been so down that you were afraid you would never come out of it? Has suicide ever been an issue for you? Great characters of the Bible apparently experienced depression including King David as he talked about being in "the depths" (Psalm 130:1) and as he wrote, "In my anguish I cried to the Lord . . . " (Psalm 118:5). Even Jesus experienced the depth of sorrow as He suffered in anguish in the garden (Luke 22:44) and as He wept over His beloved Jerusalem (Luke 19:41).

Depression is more than the occasional blue feeling that comes over all of us from time to time. Depression is a syndrome or a package of signs and symptoms that, when taken together, can be debilitating. The syndrome of depression looks like this:

Depressed Mood   -   *People generally feel sad, blue, down, or their mood is unstable and frequently goes up and down.*

Helplessness   -   *There may be feelings of being completely incapa-*

ble of changing your circumstances.

Hopelessness - *Depression can reach a point when there seems to be nothing left to hang on to and no light at the end of the tunnel.*

Guilt and Shame - *Excessive, self-punitive guilt over real or imagined past wrongdoings is often part of the picture.*

Thinking Problems - *When you are depressed you may have a greater problem thinking clearly, concentrating, and remembering things.*

Indecisiveness - *When depressed, making even simple decisions such as what to wear can be torturous.*

Self-Doubt - *When you are depressed you are apt to feel less capable, less appealing, and less worthwhile.*

Social Withdrawal - *People who are depressed often isolate themselves from friends and loved ones.*

Tearfulness - *Depression can cause either excessive crying or*

		the loss of the ability to cry.
Demotivation	-	*With depression, you have trouble getting started or following through on projects, or you may feel chronically fatigued.*
Feeling Easily Overwhelmed	-	*When you are depressed, even simple daily tasks may seem like mountains to climb.*
Pessimistic Thinking	-	*With depression, you are likely to have a gloomy outlook on yourself, your future, and most of your current circumstances.*
Loss of Meaning	-	*There may be painful questions about the meaning of life, reasons for going on, and a sense of hollowness and emptiness.*
Suicidal Thoughts	-	*Depression is often accompanied by thoughts of suicide, serious plans, and even successful attempts.*

One of the ways of looking at the syndrome that makes up depression is to look at each symptom in terms of self-esteem. In other words, how can the lack of self-acceptance contribute to the intensification of any one symptom and, conversely, how do the symptoms add to low self-esteem? Let's look at some examples. Let's say you are depressed and feeling helpless. Your low self-esteem may be blocking your ability to adequately see your gifts, talents, and God-given ability to persevere and overcome. When you are not self-accepting you may assume that others may not accept you, and consequently, social withdrawal is more likely. The demotivation in depression may be enhanced by your low self-esteem which tells you that you are unlikely to succeed anyway. The lack of self-acceptance is probably intricately entwined with nearly all the symptoms of depression.

Therefore, if you can move toward a place of greater self-acceptance, you'll have a way of treating your depression. Here is how that can happen. First of all, learn to interpret your depressive symptoms as related to your self-esteem, similar to the above paragraph. Second, learn about and understand depression as a condition that afflicts many people and stop being angry at yourself for it. Remind yourself that you did not choose to become depressed and you would shake it if you could. Next, catch yourself in the unhealthy habit of focusing on your past sins, mistakes, and failures. Remind yourself that keeping guilt and shame alive is of no benefit to yourself or anybody else. Regarding the hopeless/helpless feelings, take stock of your own internal resources and abilities to cope as well as being reminded of your eternal hope and the Lord's resources. Additionally, when feeling overwhelmed by daily tasks, let yourself fly at half-mast until you are feeling better. Give yourself permission to work at less than your potential until you start feeling better. Try to do a little more each day so that you can be reminded that you are probably more capable than you have been estimating. Finally, even before you feel up to it, reinvolve yourself socially. Socializing can be a good distraction from your lousy feelings and some positive feedback and affection can only serve to help you feel better about who you are. You may not feel worthy, but let other people decide whether they want to be around you when you are feeling low.

As you can see, addressing each of the depressive symptoms by doing what leads you closer to self-acceptance can help bring an end to depression. As you do things such as take stock in your own resources, receive positive social feedback, and give yourself grace not to work at one-hundred percent effort while you are feeling depressed, your improved self-esteem will naturally take the sting out of your anguish. It is hard to be depressed when you are truly at peace with yourself.

When you do find yourself depressed, resist bashing yourself because you are depressed. In spite of where your self-esteem might be, be self-caring enough to catch your depressive episodes early. Seek help if you need to but don't let your depression go on for too long. Finally, be sure not to let your depression lie to you about your self-worth.

Anxiety
Another problematic emotion to which most of us seem susceptible is anxiety. Anxiety is the term which we use for feelings which include tension, fearfulness, nervousness, worry, or feeling uptight and ill-at-ease. Anxiety also sometimes can include specific phobias which are irrational fears of certain objects or situations. For example, one common phobia is agoraphobia, which can sometimes lead an individual to be housebound for years. Anxiety can come in a generalized form, wherein a person feels tense, nervous, and worried most of the time. Or someone may experience

intense episodes of anxiety in the form of panic attacks. Like depression, anxiety is common and is an emotion that all of us have experienced from time to time.

The signs and symptoms associated with anxiety have both physical and psychological manifestations. When you are anxious, you may be jittery and shaky and experience "butterflies in the stomach". Your heart may pound, you may breathe more forcefully, and beads of sweat may form on your forehead. If you have ever been anxious, you may have noticed that you are jumpy and easily startled, and you may find your-self scanning the environment for potential threats. Perhaps you have felt the tightness in your chest and a smothering sensation as panic began to rise. Also common with anxiety is agitation, often in the form of pacing or needing to flee the scene or sleeplessness. People who are anxious often have trouble concentrat-ing and are distracted by racing and intrusive thoughts.

Anxiety usually includes worrying. Fearful worrying is about living in the future. Most anxiety is anticipa-tory. What this means is that if you are worried then you are projecting some awful outcome into your future. It is not uncommon for an individual to become caught up in the anticipation of the worst possible outcome and experience the same kind of fear as if that worse case scenario had indeed come to pass.

Thirty-seven-year-old Bruce had suffered from anxiety most of his life. He seemed to almost always be tense and worried about something. He installed window coverings for a living and was constantly fearful of deadlines, angry customers, and the survivability of his business. Bruce was so used to being anxious all the time, that he had virtually given up trying to calm himself down. He figured he would simply always be a "worry wart." Lately, however, his anxiety had increased to the point where he had begun to experience full-fledged panic attacks. These panic episodes usually took place while he was in his truck on the way to an installation job. Bruce would suddenly become panic-stricken and overwhelmed with a feeling that he was smothering. He focused on his heart which seemed to be pounding out of control and would become convinced that he was suffering from a fatal heart attack. In spite of reassurances from several doctors following thorough physical exams, Bruce seemed to remain convinced that his heart was about to give out. He became fearful of traveling and had trouble making himself go to work because he could never be sure when one of his panic episodes would occur. Bruce became anxiously alert to every bodily sensation and seemed convinced that even the slightest twinge was the first sign of an impending heart attack. Bruce felt embarrassed about all of his fears and sensed that his wife was losing patience with his ongoing worrying and trips to the emergency room. Intellectually, he knew that most of his fears were irrational but his awful imaginings seemed to take over. He considered himself to be weak and feared that he was crazy.

As with depression, anxiety has much to do with low self-esteem. Much of what we worry and are anxious about comes down to the fears of failure and disapproval. Bruce, for example, even though worried about death from a sudden heart attack, seemed deeply anxious about having a panic episode in public, thereby embarrassing himself. Bruce's underlying anxiety had to do with fear of failure. He was concerned about business failure and not being able to impress others with his business savvy and good income. He even felt pressured to "prove himself" to his wife. His lifelong self-doubts had opened the door to all of the self-applied pressure which, in turn, caused anxiety to build to the crescendo of panic-attacks.

Many of us, likewise, fear failure because of a strong concern of what others might think of us. We worry about disappointing others. We are afraid of looking foolish and afraid of letting people down. We avoid situations that could confirm our own self-doubts and are most anxious in settings that tap into our deepest insecurities. This is why public speaking is so frightening to many people. When self-esteem is already low, fears of failure and disapproval are intensified. People who are fully self-accepting, are less anxious because failure and embarrassment are tolerable events, no longer engendering gripping fears.

Since many of your anxieties are self-esteem related, you can reduce much of your fearfulness by addressing certain self-esteem issues. For example, if your self-esteem is low, it is likely that you place excessively high demands upon yourself to prove your worth and you may even be perfectionistic. Of course, unrealistic self-demands increase anxiety, because your chances of failure are almost certain. Self-acceptance decreases your tendency to prove your worth through success and achievement, and, therefore, the anticipation of failure fades. Anxiety may also cause you to compare yourself with others. Looking at the cool exterior of the people around you and being aware of your own insecurities and fears can cause you to chastise yourself for not being cool and calm like everyone else. Be aware, however, that everyone looks more settled on the outside than they are on the inside. Do not make the mistake of comparing the totality of yourself with the false social facade of the people around you.

154

Self-Worth Without Self-Worship

Low self-esteem also exacerbates your fearfulness because of your inability to recognize your God-given internal resources for coping. Failing to acknowledge your own strengths and ability to persevere under hardship can lead you to believe that you are more fragile and vulnerable than you really are. Self-acceptance means that you have learned to acknowledge your own internal strengths and resources which can help you to face your future. When your self-esteem is low, you are less likely to seek support with your fears and anxieties. With improved self-acceptance, you are less likely to feel embarrassed about sharing what frightens you with other people. Sometimes just talking over some of your fears with a friend can be of great benefit. Self-acceptance means that you will become self-caring enough to better address your worries before they grow out of proportion.

Decide now to stop calling yourself names and considering yourself to be weak because you experience worries and fears. Cease any anger at yourself for not being able to simply "shake it off." Jesus has exhorted us not to worry (Luke 12:22-32) but this is not to say that we are awful and unforgivable when we are fearful. Jesus simply loves us so much that He wants us to learn to trust in Him rather than worry about our day-to-day needs. He was aware of Proverbs 12:25 which says that "an anxious heart weighs a man down." Certainly God is clearly aware of our human frailty and our resulting susceptibility to being anxious and afraid. Be self-accepting in spite of your fears. The more self-accepting you are, the less fearful you will become. The less pressured you feel to be successful in order to prove yourself the more likely will be your ability to peaceably "not be anxious about anything but . . . present your requests to God" (Philippians 4:6).

155

Anger

Another problematic emotion that can be made worse because of low self-esteem is anger. Many people, especially women, feel much guilt over the anger they experience. Perhaps you believe that feeling angry makes you a bad person. Many people learned as children that anger leads to violence or somebody getting hurt. As a consequence, people can feel guilty not just in expressing their anger, but simply in feeling the emotion.

Because people with low self-esteem are more likely to deny and stuff their angry feelings, the lack of self-acceptance compounds any anger problems. Look at the case of Patty, for example. When she would become angry at her husband, she would simply withdraw and become quiet. Rather than letting her husband know how she was feeling, she would escape to another room, sometimes for several hours. This left her husband in a quandary as to what to do or say and relatively small conflicts became drawn-out fights. Due to her many insecurities, Patty felt guilty about expressing her anger and was barely able to admit that she *felt* angry. As a result, she stuffed her anger which became long-term, seething bitterness. Since she did not express her anger directly at her husband, her pent up anger showed itself in subtle and underhanded ways such as through sarcasm, irritability, and the "silent treatment." Patty swallowed so much of her anger that she literally had pains in her stomach when she became frustrated with her husband.

Increasing your self-esteem and becoming more self-accepting will help you to better manage any anger you experience. The Bible does not tell us never to become angry. Even Jesus showed strong anger (John 2:15-16). What the Bible does say, however, is that you should not sin in your anger (Ephesians 4:26). In other words, it is not the experience of anger that we need to be careful with, but rather what we do when we are angry. Stop chiding yourself about your anger. Learn to see your anger as God-given and as natural an emotion as sadness. Learn to accept yourself as a person who can feel angry. If you become more self-accepting, then you will become more appropriately assertive. This is what the Word tells you to do (Matthew 5:23-26).

The better you feel about your anger the better you will feel about yourself. The more self-accepting you are the less anger you will have because anger episodes will be shorter and you will be more likely to express you anger in an appropriate and reconciling fashion. The more guilty you feel about your anger the more likely it is that you will stuff it and turn it into bitterness.

Another important connection between anger and low self-esteem is that much anger follows from being made to feel insignificant or inferior. Preceding most anger is hurt. Most hurt comes in the form of hurt self-esteem. If your self-esteem is already low, it does not take much to tap into your insecurities, thereby resulting in hurt feelings. Ask yourself the next time you become angry with someone, how the other person's actions or words helped you to feel insignificant, demeaned, or inferior. You will find out that most of your anger is related to your own self-doubting. Self-acceptance means that you will be less likely to take things personally and, thus, be less likely to become angry.

Be accepting of yourself as a person who experiences the full range of emotions, including anger. The more accepting you can be of yourself as a person who is capable of feeling anger, the more quickly you will acknowledge your anger and express it in healthy, Biblical ways. Experiences with anger will not become buried and thus prolonged, and your relationships and self-esteem will benefit. As you increase your acceptance and understanding of your anger, your chances of sinning in your anger decline.

Lies About Your Emotions
As you struggle with problematic emotions, it is likely that you suffer from certain deceptions. Many of these lies enhance the pain that we experience with depression, anxiety, and anger. For example, you may have grown up believing that when you experience anger you are bad and, therefore, should feel guilty. Another falsehood is that experiencing depression proves that there is something defective in you. Still another lie says that you are weak and sick if you suffer from anxiety and fears. You may also be caught up in the belief that you must be "normal" and "stable" at all times. Normality is nearly impossible to define and, therefore, it becomes a vague, ever-changing target to reach. Trying to be perfectly stable will likewise be met with failure since we are all susceptible to all kinds of emotional ups and downs.

The truth is, depression, anxiety, and anger will all be a part of your human experience at one time or another. These feelings cannot be avoided. Do not be deceived into the belief that everyone else has their emotional act together simply because they look like it on the outside. This is another deception. Most people are more shaky and fragile on the inside than they allow themselves to show publicly. Stop comparing your emotional experiences with others. God created

Self-Worth Without Self-Worship

you to be fully thinking and fully feeling. Completely accept yourself as that kind of creation.

What To Do

1. Regarding depression, become aware of any false beliefs you have about it. Stop chastising yourself for your depressive experiences. Disclose to others and seek help as needed. Learn to view your depressive symptoms in terms of self-esteem and address your lack of self-acceptance in order to eliminate depression.

2. Learn to see your anxiety in terms of low self-esteem. Recognize how many of your fears are based on anticipating future failures or disapproval. As with depression, do not chastise yourself for your fears and anxieties, but rather be self-accepting enough to share with others the things that frighten you.

3. Accept yourself as a person who is capable of experiencing and expressing anger. Increase your awareness about how most of your anger is related to your self-esteem coming under attack. Learn to address the people and issues that are causing your anger in a timely fashion rather than letting your anger go on indefinitely.

4. Learn to allow your genuine feelings to emerge. Label it honestly as, for example, anger. Consider that *all* of your feelings are rational, legitimate, and acceptable. You need not feel obligated to justify each of your emotions. Use

your problematic emotions as a clue that something is wrong and that there are problems to be addressed.

5. Stop comparing your multifaceted emotional internal experiences with the superficial social facade of the people around you. Keep in mind that people look calm on the outside because they are trying to make you think they are.

6. Write out a list of how complete self-acceptance would better enable you to manage any sign or symptom from any of your problem emotions.

7. Talk to people. Tell them what you are going through and find out what similar experiences they may have had. It will be easier for you to become more self-accepting as you realize how common are many of your private experiences, including unpleasant emotional ones.

8. Memorize and meditate on the verse: "My comfort in my suffering is this: Your promise preserves my life" (Psalm 119:50).

Chapter 9
ACCEPTING YOUR BODY

"Man looks at the outward appearance, but the Lord looks at the heart" (1 Samuel 16:7).

No One Seems Satisfied
At 37, Marsha did not like what was happening with her body. Having gained only a pound or two over each of the last few years, Marsha hated herself for the extra ten or twelve pounds she was carrying. Lately she found herself fretting more and more over her appearance. She would stand and gaze at her form in the mirror and sigh with discouragement. Her mind's eye seemed to translate those extra few pounds into hips that were monstrously large. Her husband seemed to be losing patience with her increasing need to have him tell her that she was still attractive to him. He, in fact, had no complaint and barely noticed the physical changes in Marsha's body that were depressing her. Marsha herself, however, was only too aware of every new gray hair, each tiny line around her eyes, and any flaw that her microscopic searches could detect in the mirror.

Does any of Marsha's story sound familiar to you? It seems that almost no one over the age of twenty is fully satisfied with his or her own body. Self-acceptance that includes the acceptance of your physical self, is a very difficult area for many people. Do you find yourself looking in mirrors frequently? What features about your body do you most want to change? Do you ever feel disgusted with your body? Have you *ever* felt content with the body you have been given? In what ways do self-blame and name-calling come into play in your own self-talk when you reflect upon your physical appearance?

When you look in the mirror, what are you focusing on? Are there physical flaws and defects that bother you almost every time you gaze at your reflection? Do you, like many people, poke, prod, pinch, and scrutinize every aspect of your body with a highly critical eye? In general, how do you feel about your physical appearance?

Societal pressures to have a good appearance are pervasive and damaging. This seems to be especially true for women. Thinness, youth, and beauty seem to be honored to a point beyond any reason. The media implores you to focus on appearance and superficiality rather than character and spirituality.

Think of the length that people go to in an attempt to improve their appearance. Consider the hours of make-up and hair care. Millions are spent on plastic surgery that includes such techniques as liposuction. These are intrusive, painful, and expensive measures done in the interest in improving self-esteem. How unnatural and sad. To what efforts do you go to have a more attractive body? Do you spend money on tanning salons? Have you ever engaged in starvation in order to lose weight? What kinds of unpleasant exercises have you endured?

It is good to exercise, maintain a reasonable weight range, and even to comb your hair. What is not good is when your sense of self-worth is based on your internal judgment about your physical appearance. It is more healthy and meaningful to be at a point where physical appearance stops affecting your self-esteem. For example, you may be better off with those few extra pounds rather than yo-yo dieting and constantly fighting against them. You may be better off with an extra hour's sleep rather than two full hours of hair and make-up every morning. The goal is to accept yourself with an imperfect body. Then, if you decide, you can make changes because it is physically healthy rather than doing what is cosmetically prudent. The reality for all of us is that self-acceptance must take place in the context of ownership of the flawed body.

How much time and energy have you spent hating those certain things about your body? How many times have you looked at your body and then downed yourself because of it? Is your physical appearance another area where you set too high standards for yourself? With whom do you compare yourself regarding your physical attractiveness? Is it possible that you would never be fully satisfied no matter what? If your body and face were perfect, would that really be the solution in the search for self-acceptance?

> "Your beauty should not come from
> outward adornment, such as braided hair
> and the wearing of gold jewelry and fine
> clothes. Instead, it should be that of
> your inner self . . ." (1 Peter 3:3-4).

Many Problems
Your attitudes toward your body can severely impact your self-esteem. Nonacceptance of your physical self will thwart your overall efforts toward self-acceptance. As in other areas of self-acceptance, lamenting over

your physical appearance runs counter to God's way of thinking. Galatians 2:6 tells us, "God does not judge by external appearance."

But the pressure to look good can be immense. We have already talked about some expensive and even painful efforts that people go through in order to change their appearance. When you go to buy clothes and shoes, which has the highest priority, comfort or appearance. Someone once said that you have two choices in life, ugly shoes or ugly feet. Your current level of self-acceptance encourages you to choose which?

Many problems can grow out of the lack of self-acceptance for the body. For some, self-consciousness over their appearance can be a cause for great anxiety. Having to walk into a room full of people can be embarrassing because those who hate their own bodies believe that others will be equally critical of them. Hiding and withdrawing from others may result. Loneliness can follow, as those who are very self-conscious about their appearance may be afraid to initiate relationships and romances.

Being overly focused on appearance can also cause much envy and bitterness. People who are unhappy with the way they look often find themselves comparing their appearance with others. Jealousy and an even lower self-esteem are common consequences. An excessive focus on physical appearance can cause you to be more mindful of the created rather than the Creator.

If you are overly concerned about your appearance, chances are, you call yourself names such as "fat," "ugly," "old," "scrawny," or any number of other less-than-complementary terms. It is possible for you to become downright depressed simply because you hate the way you look. At the extreme, self-hatred may result. Without realizing it, you may even trash yourself for physical features which are based in genetics rather than anything you could have had any control over. Some inborn tendencies include:

> *the quality of your skin*
> *musculature*
> *tendency for weight-gain or thinness*
> *height*
> *the type of hair and balding patterns*
> *the shape of your face*
> *hair and eye color*
> *the way that you age*
> *the size and shape of your teeth*
> *breast size*
> *shape of hands*
> *hairiness*
> *where your fat tends to collect*
> *bone size and other structural aspects*
> *whether or not your bellybutton is an "inny" or*
>   *an "outy"*

Blaming yourself for any of the above God-given features makes as much sense as blaming yourself for the color of your skin. Many things about your body simply need to be accepted by you.

For some people, concern about physical appearance can become an obsession. More young women are caught up in the snare of eating disorders than you might imagine. Binging and vomiting, overuse of laxatives, and true starvation have cost the lives and health of many. Others become so obsessed about their appearance that they work on their bodies for many hours a day, for example, in weight-lifting along with the abuse of steroids. Exercise and weight control has its place, but can become compulsively out of control and dangerous.

As you reflect upon your own need to be accepting of your body, keep in mind that as your age increases so will your number of perceived physical flaws. In other words, become self-accepting about your physical appearance, or risk experiencing ever increasing unhappiness as you get older. Age means inevitable changes in body shape, a wrinkling of your skin, and increasing difficulty maintaining optimal weight. Normal aging includes a decrease in musculature and other physical changes that you may not like. But as you age, how well will your attitudes about your body reflect what Proverbs 16:31 has to say, "Gray hair is a crown of splendor"?

Fat Versus Thin
A willingness to accept your body will likely be much more difficult for you if you are overweight. That our society continues to overvalue thinness is clearly evident in the media and people's attitudes in general. Just as there is racism and sexism, there is also "weightism." This is a prejudice against people who are overweight. The problem is, however, overweight people themselves take on these prejudices and learn to hate themselves and their own bodies solely based on the presence of body fat.

Traditionally, obese people have been viewed as weak and inferior. Their obesity is often viewed as an indication of self-indulgence. The truth is, however, that the cause for obesity is basically unknown. Studies show that obese individuals generally do not consume more calories than average weight people. Studies also indicate that the composition of the meals for an obese person is no different, nor is the timing, nor is the speed of eating. The treatments for obesity generally do not work and, when they do, the weight loss usually does not last. The body is extremely reluctant to give up its extra fat. In fact, dieting may actually *cause* obesity with the yo-yo effects and alterations in body metabolism.

Since we do not clearly know the causes of obesity, and since much of it seems to be biologically based, why does being overweight have to be such a self-esteem smasher? We as a society seem to have bought into a notion of a very narrow range of acceptable body shapes and sizes. The power of the societal ideal can be shown in the generalized unhappiness that people experience with their own weight level. In a survey of 33,000 women, a popular women's magazine found that 75 percent of women questioned felt that they were too fat. Generous estimates showed that only 25 percent were overweight, and 45 percent of them were actually underweight. In order to meet ridiculous societal standards, overweight people will starve, torture their bodies, and feel terribly guilty for any dietary backsliding. There are now support groups that wisely espouse the notion of self-acceptance in the presence of extra body weight, such as the group "Full-Figured and Fulfilled." This is probably a good trend.

If you are overweight, try to begin to see that condition as more a matter of biology than the reflection of a weak will. Sure, you sometimes overeat, eat fattening foods, and even eat as a result of boredom, loneliness, or depression. Most overweight people do. But so do most thin people. Let society have its silly fears and prejudices. Does this mean you have to remain non-self-accepting simply because you put on more weight than you would like? In what ways have you been critical of yourself because of extra fat? How has society's ideal body shape affected your self-esteem?

Self-Acceptance and Self-Care

If you are lacking in self-acceptance then you may take less care of your body than you should. The Bible tells us that your body is the temple of the Holy Spirit (1 Corinthians 6:19). How do *you* take care of that temple? With low self-esteem, you may be more likely to engage in compulsive behaviors such as smoking, drinking, and overeating. Perhaps good health habits are lacking such as being sure you get enough rest and exercising regularly. Some people even deny themselves sufficient medical care, sometimes choosing to ignore pains and symptoms until it is too late.

The lack of accepting one's body can also lead to sexual sin. Promiscuity is often less the result of sexual need than it is the need to feel attractive. Many people who have basic insecurities about their own physical appeal seek reassurance through their own ability to be enticing and seductive. For some who are concerned that they are no longer attractive, the notion that someone would want to be with them sexually is irresistible. Those who are accepting of their appearance, do not need to continually prove their worth through their ability to turn heads.

Fearfully and Wonderfully Made

> "For you created my inmost being; you knit me together in my mother's womb. I praise you because I am fearfully and wonderfully made; your works are wonderful, I know that full well" (Psalm 139:13-14).

170

Self-Worth Without Self-Worship

The most important step that you can take toward the acceptance of your body is to alter the way that you conceptualize your physical being. You are indeed fearfully and wonderfully made. Learning to revel in and appreciate the complexity of the gift that is your body will help to fade your concerns over mere appearance.

If you have ever studied biology or physiology you cannot help but to be struck by the awesomeness of the creation that is your body. The creation that is you is as much a testimony to the greatness of God as any other part of creation in the universe. Learn to ponder the complexity of your body.

Reflect on how fearfully and wonderfully you have been made. For example, you have a skeletal system, a muscular system, a nervous system, an endocrine system, a circulatory system, a lymphatic system, an immune system, a respiratory system, a reproductive system, a digestive system, a urinary system, and a metabolic system, all working in coordination and conjunction at this very moment. You don't even have to think about it. It simply occurs. Aren't you clever? You're made up of 100 trillion cells. Each of these cells has a nucleus which is the brain and a kind of chemical factory for the cell. The nucleus contains the DNA which makes up 46 chromosomes and 50,000 genes. This means that every cell of your body has the blueprint for your entire body, which contains about 200 different kinds of cells. Every minute, three hundred million of your body cells die. Your body contains enough blood vessels to go around the world twice. You are made of simply water and elements such as potassium, iron, calcium, sodium, carbon, etc. Therefore, the entirety of your body is made up of water and dirt.

171

Just consider the following:

> *How do you get air and food into every cell?*
> *How does a muscle move?*
> *How can you tell hot from cold?*
> *How do you get poisons out of your body?*
> *How do you disinfect yourself?*
> *How does a McDonald's hamburger become cellular energy?*
> *How do cells know when to divide, stop growing, die?*
> *Why doesn't your heart get tired?*
> *How do we age?*
> *How do we stay at 98.6 degrees?*
> *How do the eyes see and the ears hear?*
> *How does blood clot?*
> *How can you initiate a voluntary movement?*

With all of that, why do you spend one moment worrying about the superficiality of your looks and agonize over every flaw, extra pound, pimple, or gray hair? Even if you were the most hideous looking creature in the world, you would still be the most complex machine in the known universe. Accepting your body in the wonderment that it has been made is, in a sense, a way of appreciating your heavenly Father. So stop poking, prodding, pinching, scrutinizing, and criticizing. Know more fully how fearfully and wonderfully you are made.

Self-Worth Without Self-Worship

What To Do

1.   Answer each of the following questions as they apply to you:

When you look in the mirror, what are you mostly focusing on?

What do you say to yourself regarding your body?

In what ways do you compare your body with others and are you too critical of your own?

What are the bodily flaws that have hurt your self-esteem but really have to do with genetics rather than anything for which you are to blame?

List the measures to which you have gone in order to look more attractive (don't forget clothing, hair-care, diets, etc.).

With what things about your appearance are you pleased?

2.   Catch yourself playing the comparison game. Do not allow jealousy and envy to play a role in your thought life and contribute to your low self-acceptance, especially regarding your feelings about your body. Remember that there will always be people who are stronger, more attractive, more sexy, and younger than you are.

3. When purchasing clothes and shoes make comfort, not appearance, your goal. It is better to choose ugly shoes over ugly feet.

4. Decide now to cease the harsh scrutinizing that you do of yourself in the mirror. Stop studying yourself for flaws. Realize that you are "filtering" so that you notice the flaws more than the positive features. Catch yourself in your private critical comments and self-name-calling. Remind yourself that you are more critical of your appearance than other people are and that the world does not care as much as you do about how you look.

5. Discern what is inborn, that is, having to do with your God-given genetics involving your appearance. Concede that there is much about your body that you cannot do anything about.

6. Count the cost. For example, what does your concern about your appearance prevent you from doing and how does it rob you of pleasure? How do your insecurities about your appearance affect your relationships?

7. Accept your imperfect body. Accept yourself as a whole person even with an imperfect body. This is necessary because your body will never be exactly as you would like it to be. Make changes in your physical appearance for reasons

of health and comfort rather than for purely cosmetic desires.

8.   Imagine for a moment being handicapped. Think about being blind or bound to a wheelchair. In this context, consider how much more important it is that your body functions reasonably well rather than that it has a beautiful appearance.

9.   Become aware of your own standards regarding your physical appearance. Be sure to question whether or not you are buying into society's definition of beauty which includes thinness, youth, and hard-to-achieve ideals. Learn to become more critical of what society tells you is important and less critical of yourself over your appearance.

10.   If you have concerns about being overweight, answer each of the following questions:

How has society's ideal body shape affected your self-esteem?

In what ways have you been critical of yourself because of extra fat?

How have you blamed and punished yourself for being overweight in ways that may be unfair and prejudiced?

How does your self-demeaning attitude about your weight affect your relationships?

What does your shame over your weight prevent you from doing?

If you were more self-accepting, how differently would you view your excess weight?

11. Under each statement below write three things you would do differently:

    (a) If I stopped being concerned over what others thought of my weight, I would . . .

    (b) If I no longer let my excess weight prevent me from trying new things, I would . . .

    (c) If I felt totally accepting of myself as being overweight, socially I would . . .

    (d) If I were no longer worried about or ashamed of my weight, I would stop . . .

Try out some of the new behaviors and attitudes that you wrote in the above statements. In the interest of attaining self-acceptance, behave as if you do accept yourself. If, later, you want to lose weight—fine. But first accept yourself as you are. Then decide to lose weight, not to increase your value as a human being, but because it might be a healthier or more self-caring thing to do.

12. Reflect carefully on each of the following areas of your body:

  (1) *Your feet, legs, and hips.*
  (2) *Your chest, belly and back, including all internal organs.*
  (3) *Your arms and hands.*
  (4) *Your face and head including all sense organs.*
  (5) *Your brain.*

For each area above, write the answers to these three questions:

  (a) *In what ways have you been overly concerned about appearance here and forgotten about its wonderful functions? (omit No. 5 here).*

  (b) *In what way has this area of your body served you well and brought you pleasure?*

  (c) *If you were to thank God for this area of your body, what would you be grateful for?*

Consciously learn to appreciate your body in a different way. This attitude of thanksgiving can replace your excessive concern over the superficiality of mere appearance.

13. Take time to revel in the complexity of your body. See the wonderful creation that it is and ponder some of the facts and questions about physiology that were presented in this chapter. Give thanks to God for His creative power.

14. Take some time to meditate on Psalm 139:13-14 which says, "For you created my inmost being; you knit me together in my mother's womb. I praise you because I am fearfully and wonderfully made; your works are wonderful, I know that full well."

Chapter 10

MANAGING MISTAKES

Mistakes and Self-Acceptance

If you struggle with a lack of self-acceptance, then it is likely that you carry some unhealthy notions about your own personal history of mistakes. With a low level of self-acceptance, you will normally have a low tolerance for making errors. Additionally, your memory for mistakes from your past tends to be much longer when your self-esteem is low. Without being at a place of peace about who you are, needless, self-applied guilt may be a frequent companion. Self-punishment can also result. Mismanagement of your own mistakes can lead to a separation from God. You may be forgetting the important message in John 3:17 which says, "For God did not send his Son into the world to condemn the world, but to save the world through him."

If you are like many people, you have an easier time forgiving others than you do in forgiving yourself. For example, let's say that you are talking to someone and without thinking you speak just the wrong thing at precisely the wrong moment. You hurt someone's feelings and embarrass yourself at the same time. Like most people, you would probably attempt to make fumbled, red-faced apologies and later privately berate yourself for having been "so stupid." If a friend were to tell you that they foolishly spoke something out of turn and hurt someone's feelings, would you berate them in the same way and call the friend "stupid"? Probably not. We so often think very little of someone else's bumbling boo-boo while failing to let ourselves off the hook for even minor mistakes. What is more, quite often others forgive us more easily than we forgive ourselves. Have you ever painfully confessed what you thought was an egregious error only to find that the other person shrugged off what you did as being "no big deal"?

Self-punishment, senseless guilt, and a lack of self-forgiveness is an outgrowth of low self-esteem. Keeping your awareness of your personal history of errors acutely alive is a major stumbling block toward self-acceptance. In order to help you escape the lies and sickness of low self-esteem, you must gain new perspectives and attitudes about the mistakes that you have made.

In addition to the excess guilt that you may carry over your past mistakes, fear of making future mistakes can also mean trouble. Just like with perfectionism, trying to mistake-proof your life can lead to paralysis and indecision. "What if I blow it?" "What if it doesn't turn out like I expect it to?" "What if I make a total fool of myself?" In what areas do you carry fears of personal error? Are you afraid to mess up socially, on the job, or as a parent? In what areas of your life have you failed to move forward out of fear of making mistakes?

It seems for many of us that our motto could be, "To err is human, to forget is downright next to impossible." We all know that it is okay for everybody to make mistakes, everybody, that is, except ourselves. While you may intellectually recognize the inevitability of human error even in yourself, you may behave and

180

feel deep down as if you should be truly error-free. This can lead to some pretty nasty self-talk and name-calling. "How could I have been such a fool?" "Why didn't I foresee that this was how it would turn out?" "How could I be so stupid?" "Isn't this the same dumb thing I did last week?"

There are a lot of people walking around who secretly believe that they have done the worst and been the worst. However, on the entire planet, there can only be one worst. You are probably not the one. Changing your attitudes about your mistakes will align your thinking more closely with God's because He is forgiving of you and accepts you. Without making excuses, frankly confessing what you have done wrong is part of the answer. Keeping guilt on your own head can separate you from the full knowledge of our Lord's grace, mercy, and infinite love. "If we confess our sins, he is faithful and just and will forgive us our sins and purify us from all unrighteousness" (1 John 1:9).

Mistakes Versus Sin

All error in your life has not been sin. Because of man's legalism and self-applied rigid rules, we often confuse sin with mistakes. Sin is a violation of God's law and commandments. But if you are not self-accepting, then you may treat everything that you do as a heavy moral issue. It is nonscriptural for you to consider that everything that you believe that you have done wrong represents unrighteousness in the eyes of God.

Many of us have been victimized by legalism at one time or another. While God's Word is perfect, men have distorted His Word by focusing on the "shall nots," including prohibitions not mentioned in the Bible, rather than fully recognizing God's grace

181

through the atoning power of Christ's crucifixion. Paul warned us of this unhealthy legalism in 1 Timothy 4:3-4. "They forbid people to marry and ordered them to abstain from certain foods, which God created to be received with thanksgiving by those who believe and know the truth. For everything that God created is good."

So because of legalistic teachings and also because we tend to be very hard on ourselves, those who are non-self-accepting mismanage their personal history of sin as well as mistakes by: (1) confusing mistakes and sin by feeling as if all error is in violation of God's law, (2) by failing to accept God's forgiveness for what truly is sin, and (3) by failing to let ourselves off the hook for *both* true sin and simple errors. These attitudes are a reflection of Satan's lie-filled ways, for he is ". . . the accuser of our brothers, who accuses them before our God day and night . . . " (Revelation 12:10).

In this chapter we will speak mostly of mistakes and errors but the word sin could be used interchangeably here. Many of the strategies that are provided for a healthier management of mistakes, can be likewise applied to sin. The main difference being, of course, that sin should additionally be directly dealt with through confession and seeking forgiveness through Christ. "For we maintain that a man is justified by faith apart from observing the law" (Romans 3:28).

The Facts About Mistakes
Everybody makes mistakes. While this statement may seem too obvious to be worthy of mention, it is important for you to acknowledge it as an inevitable and invariable fact. Making mistakes is a part of being human. In fact, everybody has made *lots* of mistakes. In spite of how it may feel sometimes, you have not

made the most. You have not become world champion. We have all had moments of selfishness, poor judgment, and we have all acted irrationally on occasion. You have made wrong choices, acted prematurely, or waited until it was too late. You have missed some opportunities and blown others.

Like everyone else, you have probably even done things while telling yourself that they were wrong. You have also made mistakes that have hurt others. Be especially mindful of self-punishment and a lack of self-forgiveness with errors that have caused some kind of injury to another person. Frequently, it is this kind of mistake that looms large on the list of "the unforgivable." Be aware also that everyone, like you, has made repeated mistakes. We have all engaged in some kind of shameful behavior over and over. Repeated mistakes, like any kind of error, is a part of being human.

Being human is all you will ever be. You cannot lower your value no matter how many mistakes you make. You also cannot atone for or undo everything that you have done wrong. Another problem is you are far more aware of the long list of mistakes you have made in your life and less aware of those of others. This makes for many unfair comparisons. It would be helpful to recognize that everybody has a long list of mistakes like you do and that you are safest in planning to make many more mistakes in the future. You might as well plan for this, it is going to happen.

Finally, you should know that your lack of self-acceptance can actually *cause* you to make mistakes. Consider the insecure man who finds it important to impress others and he spends his money on an expensive sports car. He later realizes that he does not have enough money left over to meet living expenses. A woman angrily snaps at her friend following what she perceived to be a critical remark, a perception which actually stemmed from her own deep feelings of self-doubt. Another example is the man who quits his long-time secure job to chase after a high-risk business venture. He ends up losing everything. His low self-esteem led him to believe that the only thing that could make him feel worthwhile was to be his own boss, make a lot of money, and have the title of President following his name. The quest for self-acceptance often leads to overly risky, irrational, and hard-to-understand behaviors that later we categorize as mistakes.

Lies That You May Believe
When self-acceptance is lacking, you are more likely to be victimized by certain lies regarding mistakes you have made in your life. For example, you might falsely believe that it is necessary and possible for you to personally atone for or undo every wrong you have ever done. In truth, atonement is often impossible and can actually cause more damage than the initial mistake. What is more, personal atonement can negate your acceptance of the atoning power of your crucifixion with Christ. Another lie that is often present with low self-esteem is the belief that you should always be able to foresee the outcome of all of your decisions and actions. The truth is, however, that many times in life you must act without knowing what the ultimate outcome might be. Therefore, calling every one of your decisions that did not work out as you had hoped a mistake, is a mistake. It is also a lie that it is possible for a human being to always act with perfect reason and judgment and to never be irrational. It is equally untrue that self-chastisement and self-punishment is always the appropriate response when you realize that

you have made a mistake. As we will see later in our discussion on self-forgiveness, self-punishment is usually a painful waste. Other lies that we often believe when we are fearful of making mistakes is the idea that we can lower our value as human beings by having a long history of blunders, that it is possible to go through life without injuring another human being, and the most common lie—that you should never make mistakes of any kind.

Other lies that we believe fly in the face of the Scriptures. Many people believe that they have done things so bad that they cannot ask the Lord to forgive them. Or, in a similar vein, they may believe deep down that what they have done is too big for God's love and forgiveness. In this way, many people continue on a track of guilt that may last for years because of their inability to accept God's willingness to accept them in spite of their sin, "Because of the Lord's great love we are not consumed, for his compassions never fail" (Lamentations 3:22).

Why Did You Do It?
When you look back on some kind of shameful behavior, you usually look directly at the behavior and forget the compelling *circumstances* that were a part of the picture at the time. For example, an otherwise cautious man decides to take the plunge and invest most of his money in the stock market. For several months the economy has been strong and people are making quick money through stocks. The man is compelled by these optimistic circumstances to "go for it" and he makes his stock purchases. Several weeks later, the market crashes and he loses most of his money. He immediately begins to berate himself for what he calls "stupidity" and "carelessness." He has completely forgotten about the circumstances surrounding his

decision, which at the time seemed to indicate that a stock purchase was sensible. Where was the mistake?

In looking back at past mistakes, you also may forget what your *state of mind* was at the time. We forget certain things like our emotional state, our self-esteem needs, youthful enthusiasm, fatigue, distraction, worry, and even strong emotions such as fear and anger. For example, have you ever been on a diet, broken that diet by eating some high-calorie, forbidden food, and then felt guilty immediately afterward? What you probably focused on and felt guilty about was the action of overeating, forgetting entirely that you were very hungry prior to this act. Since you have already eaten, the hunger is gone and quickly forgotten. At that point, you feel that it should have been easy for you to resist that slice of pie and you become self-punitive.

Finally, in looking back at past errors, you may also overlook the fact that you have more *knowledge* with hindsight than you did at the time the error occurred. For example, a mother feels guilty for not letting her son go camping with a bunch of his friends after she finds out that the camping trip went well and all had fun. In looking back she forgets that, at the time she was asked, she did not know much about the camping trip and thus did not let her son participate. When you look back, you have much more knowledge than you did at the time of the original action or decision. In looking back, you can see the future that was not available to you at the time of the alleged mistake. You almost always have more facts at hand while viewing something in retrospect.

Thus, we see the importance of looking back at the *circumstances*, your *state of mind*, and your fund of *knowledge* when you find yourself feeling bad about a particular mistake. In this way, you may tend to focus less on yourself as a defective or stupid individual and more realistically on the whole picture. Perhaps this is why the Lord God is so forgiving. He is fully aware of how compelling can be our circumstances and our state of mind. He is also aware of how limited our knowledge often is which can lead to decisions and actions which are in error.

We can conclude that the only way to never make a mistake is to not be emotion-bound (be completely just in all decisions), be able to foresee everything (be all-knowing), and be capable of controlling all circumstances and outcomes (be all-powerful). Whom do you know who is completely just, all-knowing, and all-powerful?

Self-Punishment
If you are like most people who struggle with self-acceptance, you probably have great difficulty in forgiving yourself. What you do to yourself, instead, is to self-punish. People punish themselves in a variety of ways for things that they have done wrong in the past. For example, you may work hard to keep alive the memories of past mistakes. This punishes you by forcing you to continue to feel bad about your past. You may feel especially bad for having done things in the past that wound up hurting those around you. Perhaps you feel extra guilty that you have sometimes made the same mistake over and over again. Self-punishment comes about also by keeping alive a feeling of shame inside. Guilt is what we feel when we do not like something we have done or when we have done something against God. Shame is what we feel when we do not like who we are at our very core.

Self-punishment can also come in the form of self-name-calling. Typical names you may use against yourself include "stupid," "bad," "worthless," "mean," "idiot," etc. Some people engage in self-punishment by refusing to allow themselves to have good things. One example of this might be a person who stays in an abusive relationship. A person may also refuse to seek help, including medical help, for himself or herself as another form of self-punishment. You may even find yourself failing to seek God's forgiveness even though it is always readily available to you.

Some people may engage in self-punishment by failing to take care of themselves in other ways. This may take the form of excessive drinking, risk-taking behavior, failing to take time out for pleasure or rest, or driving themselves to work too hard. You may pressure yourself to somehow "undo" or atone for what you have done in the past. As previously mentioned, it is impossible to go back and undo all of the mistakes you have made. Therefore, you must do something that will allow you to let go of your past and let go of the guilt and shame that you keep alive.

Often we continue to punish ourselves for past mistakes because we may be under the false impression that this will prevent repetition of those failures. For example, one day you tell a little white lie and feel very bad about it. You figure that in order to prevent the same old transgression, you need to keep yourself in the state of guilt and remorse over this single, relatively minor event. Other people are concerned that if they let themselves "off the hook," they will turn into some sort of immoral monster. However, just because you keep yourself feeling guilty about what you have done, does not mean that this is the only way to prevent yourself from doing it again.

Self-Worth Without Self-Worship

How can you disengage from the habit of self-punishment and learn to be more self-forgiving? This process of letting go of self-punishment begins with letting go of the past. You need to start by making a decision that self-punishment is not a good or necessary approach. You need to realize that your habit of self-punishment has gone on too long. If you feel bad about something that you did a long time ago, you may come to the realization that you have punished yourself for longer than a prison sentence might be for some serious crime. If your past mistakes include sin then take it before the Lord. Leave justice up to God and decide to let yourself be an open recipient of His forgiveness.

Self-Forgiveness
Self-forgiveness is permission to be less than perfect. Self-forgiveness can be a way of moving closer to God and enjoying more of the abundant life that He promised through His Son. Since the Lord is faithful and just to forgive, then self-forgiveness moves you into a position of being closer to the way God thinks about you.

Recognize that self-forgiveness is a positive thing. Since much of the time you cannot undo what you have done in the past, all that may be left to do is to forgive yourself. Keep in mind most self-punishment is harsh and extreme. You do not have to wait until you think you have somehow "made up for" your past mistakes in order to self-forgive. Self-forgiveness comes about through a decision that it is time to let go of your past. Be careful not to feel guilty about not feeling guilty. Finally, do not put off this important decision to forgive yourself. Self-forgiveness is one of the most important steps on the road to increased self-acceptance.

189

Here is how it is done:

1. *Recall something you did in the past that you still feel guilty or otherwise bad about. Take a separate sheet and write what you remember on the first line. Fill in the rest of the page with answers to the following questions while reflecting on this recollection.*

2. *What do you wish you would have done instead?*

3. *What were the reasons behind your doing it?*

4. *Were any of the reasons legitimate, given the circumstances at the time, your state of mind, and your knowledge? Give this question some thought.*

5. *How do you punish yourself for what you did?*

6. *How long have you punished yourself for doing it?*

7. *How much longer do you intend to punish yourself?*

8. *Whom do you help by continuing to not forgive yourself?*

9. *Are you ready to forgive yourself?*

190

10. *What if a friend told you that he or she had done the same thing? How would you feel toward that person?*

11. *Is what you did so big that God does not have the power to forgive?*

12. *If you were as willing to forgive yourself as God is, what would your attitude now be?*

Do not be afraid to self-forgive. Remember, very often it is the only thing that you can do regarding something wrong that you have done in your past. Repeat this exercise as many times as you need to for things about which you still feel guilty.

What To Do

1.   Repeat the self-forgiveness exercise from the previous section. Do it as many times as is necessary. Memorize some of the questions from the exercise so that you can quickly apply them when you catch yourself in a mode of self-punishment.

2.   Focus on the three key areas of your past mistakes—the circumstances, your state of mind, and your knowledge at the time of the mistake.

3.   Make yourself fully aware of the reality and facts about mistakes. For example, we have all made many mistakes. Even Paul spoke of this in 1 Timothy 1:15-16 when he said, "Christ Jesus came into the world to save sinners—of whom I am the worst. But for that very reason I was shown mercy so that in me, the worst of sinners, Christ Jesus might display his unlimited patience . . ."

4.   Stop self-second-guessing. It is so easy to be self-critical and look back with 20-20 hindsight at some of your past errors. Do not do this as a form of self-punishment.

5.   Brace yourself and prepare for a lifetime of mistakes and errors. God knows that you will continue to sin. That is why He sent His Son. This is not to say that you should be casual about sinful

behavior, but rather that it should be dealt with in a healing, scripturally-bound way.

6. Instead of asking why you did something or how you could have been "so stupid," ask the question, "what?" "*What* can I learn from my mistake?" "*What*, if anything, was sinful about this error?" "*What* can I learn about myself?" "*What* can be different about what I do in the future?"

7. See the humor. Not all of your mistakes are heavy moral transgressions. You do not need to take yourself so seriously. Some of what you regret from your past can actually be seen as silly and even comical.

8. Stop comparing yourself with others. You are not the world's record-holder for making mistakes. Remember, just about everyone else hides their own personal history of errors and regrettable behaviors from you just as you keep yours from them.

9. Increase your awareness of the kind of self-talk in which you engage after you have made a mistake. Do not allow any self-name-calling. Also, increase your awareness of the lies that you believe regarding mistakes.

Answer each of these questions.

> *(a)   If you were more self-accepting, how differently would you view your mistakes and shameful behaviors?*

> *(b)   Can you think of any mistakes that you have made which actually came about in your attempt to improve your self-esteem?*

> *(c)   What has your fear of making mistakes prevented you from doing?*

> *(d)   How has your fear of making mistakes interfered with your relationships?*

> *(e)   How would your life be different if you cared much less about occasionally "blowing it," messing up new projects, or having to start all over on something?*

10. Review the following list of unhealthy habits: calling myself names; attempting to control my behavior through guilt; feeling shame because I acted regrettably in the past; punishing myself with self-denial; refusing myself good things; refusing to forgive myself; refusing to accept God's forgiveness; trying to "undo" or make up for past wrongs I have done; failing to recognize that everyone has made mistakes; refusing to

"let myself off the hook." From this list, write as many "vows" or promises to yourself as you can to continue to work toward self-acceptance.

For example, "I vow to stop calling myself names," "I promise to start letting myself off the hook more readily," etc. Review these "vows" frequently as you put them into practice.

11. Make sure any mistake you have made that could represent sinful behavior is taken care of between you and God.

12. Read 2 Samuel, chapters 11 and 12. This is about David who is seen as righteous by God in spite of the fact that he committed adultery with a married woman and then murdered her husband.

13. Meditate on Exodus 34:6. Moses is speaking. ". . . the Lord, the compassionate and gracious God, slow to anger, abounding in love and faithfulness, maintaining love to thousands, and forgiving wickedness, rebellion and sin..."

195

Chapter 11
YOUR STRENGTHS AND GIFTS

You Are God's Handiwork
Like many people with a lot of personal insecurities, Jill had a habit of looking around at the faces in her church and assuming that everyone was gifted except her. A recent Sunday school discussion on the spiritual gifts had seemingly helped confirm in Jill's mind that she had nothing special to offer. Yet, as far as she could see, everyone else was terrifically gifted—smart, talented, spiritually mature, wise. If you were to ask Jill to name five positive features of herself, she would not have been able to do so. However, if you asked her to name her perceived defects, you would hear a rapid-fire litany of self-deprecation. In contrast to Jill's self-perception, her friends thought very highly of her. They knew her to be sensitive and loving, dependable and stable. Seemingly always pleasant, those who knew Jill found her warm and approachable. People simply liked to be around her.

Though she was not fully aware, Jill had a deep down sense that she was being humble and somehow "more godly" by maintaining the belief that she had no special gifts or strengths. In reality, she was simply maintaining a blindness to God's truth. The truth is, we are all gifted and the act of acknowledging our own gifts is a recognition of the Lord's love and grace in our lives. "So in Christ we who are many form one body, and each member belongs to all the others. We have different gifts, according to the grace given us . . ." (Romans 12:5-6).

Are you gifted? What are your strengths? How would you do if you were asked to name five positive personal features? Do you suffer from the kind of blindness about yourself that Jill has? Do you fail to see the fullness of God's grace in your life by failing to see your own positive features? Do you maintain a belief that it is righteous for you to privately and even publicly focus on your deficits? Do you think that it is sinful to acknowledge your strengths?

If you struggle in any way with a lack of self-acceptance, then it is quite likely that you have problems seeing your gifts. We are not just talking about the spiritual gifts as described in the 12th chapter of 1 Corinthians such as healing, tongues, faith, etc., but also personal strengths such as perseverance, courage, and talents. Some of these gifts may include artistic, musical, athletic, and communication abilities. Other strengths and gifts can include God-given features such as intelligence and other positive personality characteristics including pleasantness, compassion, and helpfulness. Gifts are also evidenced by successes such as having raised children, learning about the Lord, and your ability to treat others by God's Golden Rule.

Romans 12:3 says, ". . . Do not think more highly of yourself than you ought, but rather think of yourself with sober judgment, in accordance with the measure of faith God has given you." Obviously, we are not to esteem ourselves more highly than God would want. But it is also clear that God did not tell us to be aware only of our deficits while ignoring His grace to us through the gifts that He has given us. We are to think of ourselves in "sober judgment." Sober judgment has connotations of perception that is clear and free from distortion.

Looking at your gifts and strengths is a place of balance that helps to remove the distortions from your self-view and fight many of the lies that prevent you from accepting yourself the way God would have you do. Looking at your strengths and gifts is a way of attacking your own anti-self biases. Recognizing the positive features with which God has endowed you is not arrogance and does not include bragging or gloating. Like most aspects of self-acceptance, seeing your gifts is a private matter between you and the Lord. What we are talking about here is simple acknowledgment. It is a seeking of truth.

Acknowledging your gifts and strengths is a way of acknowledging God. 1 Thessalonians 5:18 tells us to give thanks to God in all things. Learn to see your gifts as blessings and opportunities. It is good to appreciate God's handiwork, even if that handiwork includes you.

Know that your value is not dependent upon the number and kinds of gifts that you have. You have value as God's child independent of strengths and talents. Yet, acknowledging your strengths and gifts can make you a better servant of His. Through your efforts in compassion and generosity, God can use you as His tool for answering the prayers of others. You are more likely to use that of which you are aware. You will become more bold as a servant of Christ if you confidently acknowledge that the Lord has given you gifts that He wants you to use according to His purposes.

Your Gifts

Gifts and strengths are as a much a part of being human as are making mistakes and being fallible. But if you are like Jill in our opening story, you may be struggling with recognizing and then acknowledging your own gifts. Like most people, you may need some help in the form of cues in order to see some of the good things with which God has blessed you. You will also need to remove whatever obstacles have been in the way for you, those obstacles that have kept you blind and prevented you from experiencing an unbiased, sober judgment about yourself.

As you engage yourself in the task of the acknowledgment of your gifts and strengths, be honest. Open yourself to a new understanding and recognition of your own complexity which, by design, includes a number of positive personal features. Remember, you are seeking truth, balance, self-acceptance, and things for which to be thankful. Not doing so encourages you to be depressed and anxious, and you are preventing yourself from being fully used of God.

As you discover new ways of acknowledging your giftedness, keep in mind that you will not be gifted in all areas. Some strengths that you show will not be present across all situations. But for now, you will want to focus on what is and not on what isn't. You have done enough of focusing on the negatives already. Also, keep in mind that you don't have to be great or the best at something in order to be gifted in that particular area. Many of your gifts may be quiet, low-intensity aspects of your personality that you have simply taken for granted. Quiet, hidden gifts include things like an ability to listen and a compassionate heart. Most gifts are not flashy, earth-shaking talents that turn everyone's heads.

200

Self-Worth Without Self-Worship

The next six sections will show you six different strategies to help you in your acknowledgment of the ways in which God has gifted you.

Removing Barriers

The first thing to do in your pursuit of sober judgment is to remove any barriers that may be interfering. Most of the barriers that get in the way of you recognizing your gifts and strengths have to do with distortions in your thinking and the maintenance of false beliefs. Distorted thinking such as "filtering" can cause you to feel this way. Filtering is a distortion in your thinking style in which you can easily recall defects and negatives about yourself but tend to block out talents and positive features. Or perhaps some "black-and-white thinking" is coming into play. As a consequence, you may have come to believe that if there are *some* bad things about you, then you are *all* bad. Likewise, in your black-and-white thinking, you could fail to recognize one of your talents because it is not always readily apparent. For example, perhaps you are a discerning individual who is quickly able to read other people and determine what makes them tick. But once in a while you misread someone and are completely fooled. With black-and-white thinking, you may conclude that discernment is not one of your gifts since it occasionally fails you. Yet the Word tells us that we are all gifted, and this must include you (Romans 12:5 and 6). Not all of your strengths need be invariably present in order to be representative of the gifts that God has given you. Learn to be flexible in your observance and determination of your strengths and gifts.

Sometimes the barrier to recognizing your gifts may grow out of a simple fear of seeing such gifts. Perhaps you are afraid that the acknowledgment of your gifts and strengths represents arrogance and conceit. This

201

kind of thinking is not scriptural. St. Paul himself openly acknowledged the positive things about himself. He was able to remain humble because he knew that all that he was came from God. However, there were times when he did not appear shy in his realization of the ways in which he was gifted. In 2 Corinthians 6:4-10, Paul lists some of his strengths which included: hard work, purity, patience, genuineness, kindness, sincere love, truthful speech, and righteousness. He further stated in this section of Scripture, "As servants of God we commend ourselves in every way." Paul also said in 1 Corinthians 7:7, "I wish that all men were as I am. But each man has his own gift from God; one has this gift, another has that." This is a strong comment by Paul who not only underscores the universality of God's blessings through gifts and talents, but also his unabashed yet sober judgment as he regarded himself. Fear not a frank and open search of your personality for gifts, talents, and strengths. Incessant self-deprecation is not God's will for you. False humility is a place of pride.

Another barrier to recognizing your gifts and strengths can come about through the comparison game. Like Jill, you may look around and see others as gifted far beyond yourself. Perhaps you unfairly compare your quiet and hidden gifts with someone else's "spotlight" gifts. Someone who shows talent on stage or a great gift of teaching and exhortation may be in the public eye and thus have more visible gifts. But for you to make comparisons and minimize your own gifts runs counter to the Holy Scriptures. 1 Corinthians 12:22 tells us, "those parts of the body that seem to be weaker are indispensable, and the parts that we think are less honorable we treat with special honor." Paul is absolutely clear in his teaching that one part of the body of Christ is not to be esteemed above another.

Self-Worth Without Self-Worship

Who is more important to the workings of a good church, the pastor who delivers a good sermon every Sunday or the 81-year-old widow who prays for him daily? Do not play the comparison game. See what you have and be thankful. Otherwise you may focus on what is not and be bitter.

An additional barrier to your ability to acknowledge your own gifts and strengths occurs when you base your ideas about yourself on what others think of you. As previously mentioned, your personal gifts do not need to be showy. Nor do they need to be acknowledged by others. In fact, the Bible tells us that those who appear great by worldly standards may not be used of God as much as someone who seems to be without special talent. "Not many of you were wise by human standards; not many were influential; not many were of noble birth. But God chose the foolish things of the world to shame the wise; God chose the weak things of the world to shame the strong" (1 Corinthians 1:26-27). Therefore, if you think you are foolish and weak, that is, you have no gifts, how much more can God's strength be shown in you by how you are used of Him? Your own gifts and talents need not be noticed or acknowledged by anyone else for you to accept them as truth and blessing.

Finally, you may present yourself with barriers to acknowledging your own gifts because of the too high standards you set. You may feel that you need to be great or the best at something in order to deem yourself as gifted. Perhaps you demand of yourself perfection and the use of your gifts to their fullest potential, which will actually never be possible. No one's gifts are readily present one-hundred percent of the time. Even very loving and generous people cannot demand of themselves perfect altruism every moment of every day.

203

Instead of demanding standards of perfection even in your own areas of strengths, see your gifts realistically for what they are, and with a sense of balance and purpose focus on the exhortation from 1 Peter 4:10 which says, "Each one should use whatever gift he has received to serve others." If you find yourself with the tendency to bash yourself for unmet potential and imperfect use of your own gifts and talents then try to relax and revert back to using the greatest gift of all: "Above all, love each other deeply" (1 Peter 4:8).

Praise God From Whom All Blessings Flow
One of the ways of identifying your gifts is to count your blessings. Take just a moment to answer how you have been blessed in each of the following areas of your life:

> *friendships*
> *family relationships*
> *marriage*
> *as a parent*
> *in your work life*
> *in your home life*
> *in your leisure activities*
> *in your church life*
> *in your compassion and the way you treat others*
> *in your good habits and self-discipline*
> *in your spiritual life*
> *in your body*
> *in your moral life*
> *in your ability to cope and to persevere*

If you stop to think about it, many of the blessings that you counted above are actually reflections of gifts, special talents, skills, and positive character features that you have. For example, let's say that you counted several blessings in your church life. Some of these blessings may come about and be indicative of your own willingness to help, your tendency to be cooperative, and your general friendliness. While God may have blessed you with a wonderful church and fellow Christians, he may also have blessed you with certain gifts that help you to enjoy such blessings through the giving of yourself. Another example might be that God has given you the ability to be self-disciplined in some area of your life, for example, in your work life. Thank Him for that gift and acknowledge that self-discipline is a positive part of who you are and how He made you. Review your generated list of blessings and see if you can translate some of those into personal gifts and strengths.

How You Are Used Of God
Another way of discerning your positive personal features is to focus on how God has used you to serve others. Now you may not be a minister by profession, but it is likely that you have had some positive impact on someone, somewhere along the line. Take some time to reflect upon how you have been used to:

teach
comfort
solve problems
give of yourself
give of your time
give of your money
give of your effort
strengthen
exhort
edify
support
cheer and uplift
nurture
heal

*illustrate God's presence in your life
witness the gospel of Jesus Christ*

Has God in anyway used you to meet the needs of those He loves? Do not minimize even the smallest of efforts and moments of support that you have given to others. This is how God has chosen to use you.

As you are counting the ways that God has used you to serve others, think about how you have been His servant in large or small ways in all arenas of life such as your job, your church, your neighborhood, your home, your school, and your community at large. Just as you learned with the blessings, each of the ways that you have noted that God has used you can be seen as representative of your gifts, talents, and strengths. For example, let's say that you now recognize that God has used you to edify others. This might represent thoughtfulness and compassion on your part. Perhaps the Lord has used you in the function of nurturing others. Positive characteristics that may be present in this case could include selflessness, sensitivity, and generosity. Maybe you have helped a number of people solve problems. In this way, you could count intelligence, wisdom, and discernment as some of your gifts from God.

A Great Friend
Now let's shift for a moment to looking at the characteristics of your friends. Think about friends that you have, have had, or would like to have. What do you love about these people? What kinds of things do you appreciate most in your friends and look for when you are making new friends? If you wrote out a list of what you appreciate most in your friends, it might look something like this:

> *honest*
> *high integrity*
> *dependable*
> *unconditional positive regard for you*
> *sense of humor*
> *fun*
> *supportive*
> *good listener*
> *loyal*
> *sensitive*
> *even-tempered*
> *pleasant*
> *helpful*
> *generous*
> *caring*

A person who has all of the above features would be a wonderful individual indeed. This would be someone who would be easy to love. Someone you would want to be around. Someone who would likely bless your life in many ways.

Now if you were really honest with yourself, in looking at the above list of positive features that you would love in a friend, how many of those features do you have? Probably you do not have them all and probably you do not have those features with unwavering consistency. Yet, if you ask yourself, aren't you generally willing to offer things such as honesty, good listening, caring, and dependability in your relationships? When you have a friend in need, do you not try to be helpful, supportive, and loving? If you love these characteristics in a friend and can count them as his or her special gifts, can you now acknowledge your own giftedness in some of these characteristics?

Multiple Choice
One of the best ways to be cued in on your strengths
and gifts is to work from a ready-made list from which
to pick and choose. Looking at a list of positive
personal features and identifying those that may belong
to you may seem awkward at first. This awkwardness
that you feel just shows how unaccustomed you are to
acknowledging your own strengths. Below is provided
a list of positive human features and gifts in order to
help you identify those that belong to you. Place a
check mark beside each one that you are able to show
at least some of the time. Remember, you cannot have
every gift there is and those that you do have may not
manifest themselves one-hundred percent of the time.
Be grateful and thankful in your acknowledgment of
any item you have from the following list:

A.   **Area of relationships**
caring
supportive
loving
affectionate
considerate
loyal
good listener
giving
complimentary
faithful
avoid conflict
nice
treat people well
concerned about others' feelings
able to put others first
thoughtful
kind
gentle
concerned about others' problems

208

pleasant
come through when others need help
fun
able to compromise
care about sexual needs of spouse
good friend
respectful

B.   **Area of morality and spirituality**
honest
generous
sensitive
discerning
concerned with social problems
wise
faithful
spiritually-minded
trustworthy
committed to God
healing
prophetic
moved by the suffering of others
try to do the right thing
courteous
good teacher
try not to hurt others
humble
thankful
fair with others
spiritually-gifted
not racially prejudiced

C.   **Area of maturity and responsibility**
responsible
dependable
reliable
mature

keep promises
good parent
hard working
good spouse
contribute to family finances
good housekeeper
good cook
flexible
good employee
good administrator
organized

D. **Miscellaneous areas**
attractive
used to be a good child
can tolerate hardship
generous with possessions, money, time
intelligent
curious
accepting of others' faults
skilled in your profession
masculine
feminine
creative
artistic
likable
musical
athletic
good sense of humor
do nice things for others
original and nonconforming
good brother or sister
socially skillful

Do not worry if your list is short or long. Focus on what is rather than on what is not. Again, be thankful for what He has given you. Remember your list, review it frequently.

Elaboration
Take the list of items that you checked in the above section and write them out on paper. This time, rather than just listing them, you are to elaborate on them. Describe how God has allowed you to use each of your gifts in various areas of your life. Give examples, evidence, and illustrations of those positive qualities that you have discovered. For example, if you believe that you are a dependable person then you might write, "I am dependable. When I am asked to do something, I usually follow through. For example, when I agreed to teach a Sunday school class, I did not miss one Sunday morning in two years. Also, several people have mentioned that I can be depended on."

You may write anything about yourself as long as it is positive. Use as much elaboration and as many examples as you possibly can. What you want to end up with is a decent essay about yourself. Do not consider writing about yourself in this way as a lack of being humble. Rather, see it as honest acknowledgment of the truth about the fullness of who you are as a human being and a child of God. Enjoy your essay. Put it somewhere where you will see it everyday. Read over it at least once per day. If you go to all of the work of generating the essay, and discover what God has given you, then get as much mileage out of it as possible. Reading and rereading your work here is an important step in simply regearing all of the negative thinking you have done for many years.

Some Final Questions
As you now know, people have a tendency to carry with them internal barriers that prevent them from

seeing their positive features.   One way of working around this phenomenon is to answer questions that are specifically designed to get you to focus on your gifts and strengths.   A host of tasks is provided below. Resolve to respond by jotting a quick answer to each one and to reflect upon the legitimacy of your answers. Your answers will be affirming and compatible with truth and your goal of becoming more self-accepting. Your distorted and negativistic thinking has dominated for too long.   It is time to give the truth a chance.

1.   *Say something positive about your ability to cope with problems.*

2.   *If you have a job, say something positive about the way you treat your co-workers.*

3.   *If you have children, name a way that you have sacrificed for them.*

4.   *Name something at which you have succeeded.*

5.   *Name something that happened that helped you to be more self-accepting.*

6.   *If you are married, name something your spouse likes about you.*

7.   *Name a positive change that you have made in yourself in the last few years.*

8.   *Say what you would do if a friend came to you with a personal problem.*

9. *Finish this sentence: "If I weren't so critical of myself, I would . . . "*

10. *Name something you worked hard for.*

11. *Give an example of how you are dependable at work.*

12. *Name a time when you were courageous enough to ask for help.*

13. *Say something about your ability to be accepting of others.*

14. *Name the subject that you know the most about.*

15. *Name a time in your life when you showed perseverance or the ability to "stick with it."*

16. *Name something at which you are good.*

17. *Name ways in which you believe you have good moral values.*

18. *Name a time when you cared about how someone else was feeling.*

19. *Tell about a time when you put someone else's wishes ahead of your own.*

20. *Say why you think other people would be glad they met you.*

21. *Name something about your body of which you should be more accepting.*

22. *Name an area in your life in which you have shown real commitment.*

23. *Name a person by whom you feel accepted.*

24. *Tell about the most difficult job you have ever done.*

25. *Finish this sentence: "Even though I have not accomplished everything I would like, I have managed to . . . "*

26. *Name a special circumstance from your past or in your present that makes it even more amazing that you do as well as you do.*

27. *Name something smart that you have done for your health.*

28. *Name a time when you were honest about something even though the circumstances made it difficult for you to tell the truth.*

29. *Name something that is difficult, but you do because it is the right thing to do.*

30. *Say why your age is a good age to be.*

31. *Name something positive you would like to have written on your tombstone.*

32. *Name something about your behavior that you think is good.*

33. *What is the one thing that you like to be complimented on the most?*

34. *Say something positive about your family.*

35. *Finish this sentence: "One area for which I have trouble giving my self credit is . . . "*

36. *Tell about a time when you helped someone else become more self-accepting.*

37. *Say something positive about the way you treat others.*

38. *Say something about your sensitivity toward others.*

39. *Name one of your gifts or strengths of which you need to be more aware on a daily basis.*

40. *Name something that you once taught someone else.*

41. *In what ways are you courteous?*

42. *Name something that you like about your character.*

43. *Name a time when you made a good decision about something important.*

44. *Say in what ways are you a good listener.*

45. *Finish this sentence, "I have made many mistakes, but . . . "*

46. *Say how you are trustworthy.*

47. *Name a way that you have shown strength through hardship.*

48. *Say something positive about the kind of child you were.*

49. *Say something positive about your response to God.*

50. *Name a skill that you have.*

51. *Name some ways that you have been obedient to the Lord.*

52. *Finish this sentence: "I may not be the perfect person but . . . "*

53. *Describe how you have grown in your faith.*

Decide to read no further until you have written a response to all of the above items. You will be amazed that how doing so can help you on the road toward self-acceptance. Make sure that you have firmly decided that it is good to acknowledge the strengths and gifts that you have.

Self-Worth Without Self-Worship

What To Do

1. Be sure that you have counted and acknowledged your strengths and gifts from the six final sections from this chapter starting with the section on barriers. Remember, reflect upon, appreciate, and use your gifts.

2. Count the costs. Think about the ways in which your lack of understanding of your own giftedness has caused you pain, sorrow, and loss. Count the cost to your faith and your relationship with the Lord. Think of the things that you may not have attempted because you did not realize some of the ways that God gifted you.

3. Pretend that you do not have low self-esteem and are *fully* self-accepting. What would you then notice about your own strengths and giftedness?

4. Ask a close friend what he or she thinks your gifts are. Ask him or her frankly what is liked about you and what he or she believes some of your strengths are.

5. Pretend that someone has just interviewed your family, co-workers, and friends regarding you. If questioned about your personal strengths, talents, positive features, and other qualities, what would be noted? Remember, these people probably would not be as unfairly critical of you as you are of yourself.

6. Firmly decide now that it is okay for you to acknowledge your strengths. Make yourself fully aware that recognizing who you are, including the good things that God has given you, is a way of seeking the truth.

7. Let yourself be less than perfect in the use of your gifts. Do not put yourself down because of inconsistencies and incompleteness in the way you use your gifts and talents. Remember, no one meets his or her full potential.

8. Review your written list of strengths and thank God specifically for each one. Then ask Him how He would like to use you and those gifts in His service. Keep asking until you know what the answers are.

9. Memorize and meditate on this verse: "Now to each one the manifestation of the Spirit is given for the common good" (1 Corinthians 12:7).

Chapter 12
SELF-ACCEPTANCE THROUGH AFFIRMATIONS

This Thing Called Self-Acceptance

Self-acceptance is the goal. Helping you to reach this goal is the entire purpose for this book. Self-acceptance means seeing and acknowledging the truth. "By wisdom a house is built, and through understanding it is established; through knowledge its rooms are filled with rare and beautiful treasures" (Proverbs 24:3-4). Coming to a place of self-acceptance is an important component to spiritual warfare. Self-acceptance is coming against lies and he whom Jesus called "the father of lies" (John 8:44).

Since we are talking about the acknowledgment of truth, then to become self-accepting must include the taking on of God's view of you. In your considerations regarding the issue of accepting yourself more fully, you should be in prayer about what God would want you to know about this critical issue. Your prayer might mirror David's when he wrote, "Show me your ways, O Lord, teach me your paths; guide me in your truth and teach me, for you are God my Savior, and my hope is in you all day long" (Psalm 25:4-5). In that same Psalm, David acknowledges, "Good and upright is the Lord; therefore he instructs sinners in his ways. He guides the humble in what is right and teaches them his way" (Psalm 25:8-9). You see, God does not

219

worship you but He does accept and love you enough to want to teach and guide you.

Later in the Scriptures, Paul tells us that if we allow our minds to be renewed by God, that is, to become more in tune with His truth, then we are more likely to be living within God's will. If the lack of self-acceptance is based in lies, and this causes you to be self-centered such that you are not the servant God intended you to be, then self-acceptance can free you to do and be what God wants. "Do not conform any longer to the pattern of this world, but be transformed by the renewing of your mind. Then you will be able to test and approve what God's will is—his good, pleasing and perfect will" (Romans 12:2).

Self-acceptance means that you must "think of yourself with sober judgment" (Romans 12:3), which includes a full acknowledgment of your flaws and weaknesses as well as your strengths and gifts. Self-acceptance must include the acceptance of the entire package as designed by God. When you become more self-accepting you then eliminate the need for defensiveness, overcompensation for perceived defects, perfectionism, and all of the other ills and conflicts that come about from self-dislike. You will become less defensive, perfectionistic, etc., since you will have already frankly assimilated the truths of your imperfections, the truths of your fallen nature, while still being able to see yourself through God's eyes.

Self-acceptance means learning to accept yourself as easily as you do others. It means to accept yourself based upon your being and your beliefs rather than what you are doing and what you have been trying to earn. Remember, you cannot do enough to earn your value.

Self-Worth Without Self-Worship

What gets in the way of your own self-acceptance? What have you been waiting for before you allow yourself to experience the healthy position of complete acceptance of yourself? What have you designated as your personal "point-of-arrival"? How many pounds do you need to lose, how many promotions must you gain, how many material possessions do you need to collect before you will decide to let go of the lies that have kept you in chains? There can be no "point-of-arrival" except for that moment when you came to know Jesus Christ as God's true Messiah and accepted Him as your very own. For the Word tells us that you will remain incomplete unto yourself though God is working on you this very moment. "Being confident of this, that he who began a good work in you will carry it on to completion until the day of Christ Jesus" (Philippians 1:6).

Stop waiting for something to happen before you will allow yourself the peace of self-acceptance. Your lack of self-acceptance is a way of denying the wonderment that is God's handiwork. For God himself looked at all that He had made, including humankind, and saw that "it was very good" (Genesis 1:31). As we learned in the previous chapter, self-acceptance is a way of worshiping God through the thanksgiving of the life He has given to you. Let your self-acceptance encompass the full knowing that you are just a person who has weaknesses, moments of selfishness and anger, areas of sin, and times of indulgence. This does not mean that we should not give great attention to the sinful areas of our lives. Rather, it is knowing and accepting yourself fully while He who created you is completing the good work He began.

Using Affirmations

It should be clear by now that self-acceptance comes about through the acceptance of truth. This is where affirmations come in. Affirmations are truthful statements. As the name implies, affirmations are affirming and truthful. Affirmations are full of grace and forgiveness. They are realistic and reasonable in what they encourage you to be and to do. The most important affirmations, as you will see, are what God has said about you as a believer.

Self-acceptance is enhanced through letting affirmations replace the lies that you have believed about yourself and, thus, undoing the distortions in your thinking. Affirmations help by altering your internal dialog.

We're not talking about the power of positive thinking. Statements that tell you that you are "wonderful," "great," and "can do anything you set your mind to do," are not helpful because they are not fully based in truth. But affirming statements that tell you that being average is okay, that no one ever reaches their fullest potential, and that you are loved by God anyway, can help to ease much of your self-applied pressures because such statements are based in truth and, therefore, are more reasonable and realistic. It is *realistic* thinking that has power, not positive thinking.

We will take a look at two different kinds of affirmations. The first type, which will be represented in a series of paragraphs, is a set of common-sense, gentle statements and attitudes. These affirmations represent, for most of us, a sharp contrast to the way we typically talk to ourselves. These affirmations represent more reasonable self-talk and include healthy promises that you make to yourself.

Self-Worth Without Self-Worship

The second set of affirmations that is provided later includes statements taken directly out of the Scriptures. These are statements about who you are as a believer and they highlight your position in Christ. These statements are absolute truth about how God views and values you.

Read the affirmations slowly and out loud. Think about what you are reading and reflect upon each statement. Accept the truthfulness of each affirmation even though it may be something that you have never before believed. Let each affirmation wash over you and become a part of you. What you want is for the affirmations to become a part of your new internal dialog.

General Affirmations

I am a person of value and worth. I was created by God and given value through Him. My worth does not decline throughout my life, it remains the same. Only my feelings about my worth can change. My value and worth is the same as that of anyone else. I will no longer allow the lies in my life to force me to believe otherwise.

I was once a very young and innocent child. I had the same worth and value as any child. That value did not disappear the day I became an adult. Growing up does not mean growing into worthlessness. God loved me when I was a child and He loves me now in exactly the same way.

When I was a child I may have received a message that I was somehow bad or not good enough just being me. Whether I was told that I was not good enough or I assumed that this was so, does not matter. What matters is that I believed something that was a lie.

223

Simply because I was imperfect as a child does not mean that I cannot appreciate who I was when I look back at my child-self. I am willing to take an honest and even painful look at my childhood. If seeking truth means that I may have to view some aspects of my parents in an uncomplimentary fashion, I will do it, without guilt. Seeking truth about my childhood does not dishonor my mother and father.

I will seek to be motivated by goals other than worldly prestige and status. What God wants me to do with my life is the most important thing that I could do. I will refuse to be overly critical of myself and appreciate the uniqueness of both myself and others. I will express my opinions and feelings in an honest, though thoughtful manner. I will be unafraid of new endeavors in spite of the possibility of failure. I will attempt to be more socially involved and handle criticisms and compliments with grace. As my self-esteem improves, I will be freer from resentments, jealousies, and the need for demanding attention. I will, therefore, be a better servant. As I exchange lies for truth, I will be more at peace with who I am and be free to better use my energy to give to others.

I recognize that many of the standards for which I strive come from man and not from God. Many of these standards are unreachable and fail to provide the benefit that is implied within each one. I will alter my standards to be more in line with what is realistic and with what God wants for me. My expectations of myself are now becoming more reasonable and flexible. I will no longer accept self-applied labels that come about through the failure to reach unrealistic standards. When I fail, I am not a failure. When I behave foolishly, I am not a fool. When I do not get enough work done, I am not necessarily lazy.

224

Self-Worth Without Self-Worship

I will no longer strive with overwork and unhealthy expectations toward some goal in an effort to feel better about myself. I will not try to be more than simply human. Simply human is what God made me to be. Life is short. It is not a contest that I must win. On this earth, I cannot expect to ever fully "arrive."

I will learn to become more critical of my thinking and less critical of me. Being more critical of my thought-life allows me to be more aware of the lies to which I adhere and the differences between the way I think of myself and the way God thinks of me. By looking critically at my own thoughts, I can renew my mind and prevent unhealthy thinking from running away with itself and causing me to view myself in a distorted fashion. I will become more aware of the distortions and biases in my self-view. I will change the labels that I now apply to myself and reframe my thinking so that it is more gentle and balanced.

Because my life is so full of mistakes, it is not possible for me to atone for everything that I have done. I cannot turn back the clock and undo all wrongs that I may have committed against others. I fully recognize my absolute need for the atoning power of the cross. I will no longer delay self-acceptance because of my inability to atone for the things that I have done wrong. Through confession and the acceptance of God's forgiveness, I will let go of needless guilt and try to learn from my past mistakes. Also, since self-atonement is impossible, the only thing that may be left for me is self-forgiveness. I will curtail any self-punitive thoughts or actions. Because of my increased awareness of the absurdity and senselessness of self-punishment, I will now begin to treat myself as kindly as I might a close friend.

225

I will engage in at least occasional self-care without guilt or feeling selfish. Self-denial is important only when done in a balanced and reasonable fashion. Self-denial is not always the most moral thing to do. My heavenly Father also wants me to do what is healthy for my own physical, mental, and spiritual life. Taking time for myself and engaging in rest and pleasure may be the best thing that I can do for others. Self-care is not the same as self-centeredness. Even very generous people take time for themselves.

Since I probably do not have everyone fooled anyway, I am going to choose to more generally expose who I really am. Being genuine with others means being more who God made me to be. Being genuine leads to greater intimacy with others. I will show more of the real me in spite of the fact that others may not like me. Putting up a good front at all times is too exhausting. If I let others get to know the real me and they like me, then we have a basis for a truly strong relationship. I do not always have to make a good impression. It is likely that other people will not reject me in the same harsh ways that I have rejected myself. From now on, I will be more genuine with others.

I will now try to live in the present moment. I will become aware of the richness of God's world around me with the sights, sounds, and interactions that are a part of my day-to-day experience. I will no longer allow my lack of self-acceptance to keep me focused on regrets of the past. Likewise, my low self-esteem will no longer keep my head in the future, worrying about what might go wrong.

My value as a human being is actually entirely independent of my appearance. It is petty and superficial to base my sense of self-worth on the appearance of my body. I will probably never be completely happy with all aspects of my physical appearance. I will learn to be more thankful for the body that the Lord has given to me. I must learn to accept flaws and imper-fections in my body. I do not have to look good. I am probably far more aware of my physical flaws than anyone else would ever be. Extra body fat, no matter how much, is not a measure of my worth. The degree to which I look old is not a measure of my value. It is probably not worth all the expense, trouble, and pain that I have gone through in efforts to improve my looks. I live in my body, but I am not my body. I will now stop chastising myself over every physical flaw, extra pound, or wrinkle. I will no longer use the mirror as a place to stand and mentally highlight all of my physical imperfections. God looks at the heart of a person and cares nothing about external beauty.

I will become more aware about how the actions of others are dictated by the management of their own self-esteem. I will now take into account that when people do things that I do not like, they are responding to their own insecurities. This will allow me to be more understanding and, consequently, more forgiving of others. I will see others as victims of their own low self-esteem and of lies about who they are. I will now be less critical of others around me. I will do what I can to edify others. Because everyone is struggling privately in his or her own way, I will not take so personally everyone's reactions to me.

Now is the best time for me to seek truth and to become self-accepting. Self-acceptance is not the same as arrogance. People who appear to be arrogant or prideful probably have low self-esteem and, therefore, have to resort to bragging and other related behaviors to compensate. Self-acceptance actually shows itself in the quietness of inner peace. Honestly acknowledging my gifts and talents is not the same as conceit. Being constantly self-critical is not the same as humbleness. I will allow myself to become more self-accepting. Self-acceptance is a healthy and worthy goal for which to strive.

I will stop trying to be more than just a human being. I will be only that which God created me to be. I will allow myself to be just a person with all of the weaknesses, failures, and moments of selfishness that go along with being human. God understands this, and so will I. It is all right for me to sometimes indulge, make mistakes, waste time, disappoint others, change my mind, dream, be inadequate, and present a poor image. I can always try to improve myself but, for now, I accept myself for who I am today in much the same way that God does.

How did you feel as you read through the above paragraphs? Did you notice that the gentle and accepting tone brought about a feeling of peace and comfort? Which of the above paragraphs did you find most personally helpful?

Your Position As A Child Of God
The following affirmations are Scriptures that very simply and directly tell you who you are in God's eyes as a believer in Christ. By becoming intimately acquainted with these truths, you will be able to experience what Paul wished for us when he encouraged us, "to be made new in the attitude of your minds; and to put on the new self . . ." (Ephesians 4:23-24). Imperfect though you may be, you are created by God Almighty and, just as the apostle Paul, you are loved by God through the eyes of grace. "But by the grace

Self-Worth Without Self-Worship

of God I am what I am, and his grace to me was not without effect" (1 Corinthians 15:10).

If you are a believer in Christ this is who you are:

Christ counts you amongst His friends (John 15:15)
You were chosen by Christ (John 15:16)
You have peace with God (Romans 5:1)
You have access to the grace of God by your faith (Romans 5:2)
You are reconciled to God (Romans 5:10)
You are saved through Christ's death and resurrection (Romans 5:10)
You will be united with Christ in His resurrection (Romans 6:5)
You are dead to sin (Romans 6:11)
You are alive to God in Christ Jesus (Romans 6:11)
The Holy Spirit is in you (1 Corinthians 6:19)
Your body is the temple of the Holy Spirit (1 Corinthians 6:19)
You were bought at a price (1 Corinthians 6:20)
You are blameless in God's eyes (1 Corinthians 1:8)
He has given you many great and precious promises (2 Peter 1:4)
You have a divine nature (2 Peter 1:4)
You will receive a rich welcome into the eternal kingdom (2 Peter 1:11)
God's power is at work within you (Ephesians 3:20)
You are the body of Christ (1 Corinthians 12:27)
You are God's workmanship (Ephesians 2:10)
You are raised up with Christ and seated with Him in the heavenly realms (Ephesians 2:6)

You are a member of God's household (Ephesians 2:19)
You are an heir with Christ (Ephesians 3:6)
You are seen as truly righteous and holy (Ephesians 4:24)
You are a new creation (2 Corinthians 5:17)
He did not spare His own Son for you (Romans 8:32)
Christ is interceding for you at the right hand of God (Romans 8:34)
You are more than a conqueror (Romans 8:37)
Nothing can separate you from God (Romans 8:39)
You are a son of God (Romans 8:14)
There is no condemnation for you (Romans 8:1)
You are a saint (Ephesians 1:1)
You are beloved of God (Romans 1:7)
You are the light of the world (Matthew 5:14)
You are victorious (1 Corinthians 15:57)
You have direct access to God the Father (Ephesians 2:18)
You are near to God (Ephesians 2:13)
You are reconciled to God (Ephesians 2:16)
You are qualified to share in the inheritance of the saints (Colossians 1:12)
You are holy in His sight (Colossians 1:22)
You are made complete (Colossians 2:10)
You were buried with Christ and are now raised with Him (Colossians 2:12)
You are completely forgiven (Colossians 2:13)
You can confidently approach God's throne to receive help (Hebrews 4:16)
You are accepted (Romans 15:7)

These powerful truths are from God and pertain specifically to you as a believer. It is directly out of the Bible and it applies right now. Though these truths may be unfathomable to us, they are, nonetheless, undeniable and for all eternity. Have you yet to take in the full meaning of what the Lord God did for you 2000 years ago? Are you willing to begin to try to accept who you really are through His matchless grace?

What To Do

1.　Answer these questions.

What gets in the way of your self-accept-ance?

What are the differences in the way that you accept yourself versus the way you accept flaws and mistakes in others?

What have you been waiting for or been wanting to happen before you allow complete acceptance of yourself?

How would your life be different if you were completely self-accepting?

2.　Count the costs. Think about what your lack of self-acceptance has cost you in terms of joy, relationships, your work life, and your walk with the Lord?

3.　Count the benefits. In what ways could your service to others and your relation-ship with the Lord be improved if you both recognized your weaknesses and counted your gifts and then became more self-accepting?

4.　On a separate sheet, write a finish to this sentence: "If I were more accepting of my character, I would . . . " Do this four times and include the first part of the statement each time. For example, you might write, "If I were more accept-ing of my character, I would learn to

232

appreciate what a nice person I am."
Or, "If I were more accepting of my
character, I would not put myself down
for being less than perfect."

Then do the same with this sentence:
"If I were more accepting of my body,
I would . . . " For example, "If I were
more accepting of my body, I would not
be so obsessed about a few extra
pounds." Do this four times.

Next, complete this sentence: "If I were
more accepting of what I have done in
the past . . . " Do this twice.

Next: "If I were more accepting of my
faults, I would . . . " Do this twice.

Next: "If I accepted myself the way
God accepts me, I would . . . " Do this
twice.

Read over your completed work many
times. Take on an attitude of self-acceptance. Change some things about
yourself if you would like, but accept
yourself first, right where you are today.

5. Describe the contrast between the content of the affirmation paragraphs in this
chapter and the way you talk to yourself.

6. Read and reread the affirmations in this
chapter. Make extra copies of the affirmations and place them in prominent
places where you are likely to see them
many times each day. Repetition here is
the key. Read the affirmations and the
affirming Scriptures until they become
more a part of you.

7.   Take a separate sheet and write out ten affirmations from the chapter which would most likely help you on the road to self-acceptance. Read this list frequently, at least twice per day. Reread it until you practically have it memorized. Think about what it is saying each time you read it. Open yourself up to a whole new attitude. Remember, repetition is the key since you are fighting years of habitually talking to yourself in ways that give you little grace and self-regard.

8.   After rereading the scriptural affirmations, write out several responses to this question: What is it that I most need to realize about God's love for me?

9.   Memorize and reflect upon this verse in which God is speaking to you: "I have loved you with an everlasting love; I have drawn you with loving-kindness" (Jeremiah 31:3).

Chapter 13
PUTTING ON
THE
NEW SELF

Insight Into Action

To finalize, solidify, and bring to full fruition the learning that you have gained from this book, it is imperative that you accept the challenge of turning your insights into action. Perhaps you now realize, for example, that approval and achievements generally do not aid you in your endeavors for self-acceptance. Nor are they necessary in order for God to accept you. You may have also come to realize that perfection is impossible. You may even be able to identify some of your own strengths and gifts. These elements of new learning are called insights. For our purposes, insights are important realizations and discoveries, especially about yourself. Insights enhance the renewing of your mind. But insights become most fruitful only when they are translated into new ways of behaving. Insight into action is living out what you have learned.

Insights can help you to think more clearly, be aligned with God's attitudes, and to feel better, but this is only the beginning. When new understanding leads you to act differently, at least two important things occur. First, your insights will produce much more fruit. For example, let's say your attitudes about your productivity have changed. You now realize that perfectionism and workaholism are pointless and unhealthy. If you *live out* these new attitudes then you might spend less time on the job and more time with your children, your spouse, and your friends. You would also naturally have more time for rest and fun—a more balanced and abundant life. The second thing that occurs as you turn insight into action, is that it accelerates your reaching the goal of self-acceptance. Again, using our example of the perfectionistic workaholic, you would gain additional helpful insights in the new, more relaxed life style, such as the realization that resting and spending time with the family is just as important as being productive on the job. Or, you may become more self-accepting as you enjoy your new identity as a family-oriented individual.

Insight into action is about changing from the outside in. Sometimes, in order to *feel* differently you have to *do* something different. In order to think more clearly, you often have to try new ways of living. In order to gain understanding, it is sometimes necessary to wear different hats and try new roles. In the same way that faith without works is dead, so is insight dead without manifest change.

The Word tells us, "To be made new in the attitude of your minds; and to put on the new self . . ." (Ephesians 4:23-24). What is this new self? The new self is to fully be who God made you (1 Corinthians 15:10). The new self should also be helpful to others, building them up (Ephesians 4:29). The new self should include kindness and compassion for one another and a willingness to forgive (Ephesians 4:32). Being kind and forgiving, as has been shown throughout this book, is more likely to occur in the wake of self-acceptance and self-forgiveness. Putting on the new self means to put off falsehood and to speak truthfully (Ephesians 4:25). Insight into action means learning to fully be exactly who you were meant to be.

Self-Worth Without Self-Worship

This chapter contains three basic strategies for changing your insight into action and to live out what you have learned. These three strategies are:

1.   *Letting Go*
2.   *Life Experiments*
3.   *Learning to be Genuine*

Each of these three techniques will be described in detail below. Try each one for yourself. Then sit back and watch the fruit of your new self as it emerges.

Letting Go

The phrase "letting go" means different things to different people. It could mean: letting yourself be imperfect, letting others be in charge, doing things in a sloppy fashion sometimes, allowing others to not like you, not controlling all the feelings that you have, letting go of self-defeating persistence, not meeting others' expectations, and not being overly responsible. Letting go may mean letting someone else and letting the natural consequences of events run their full course. Letting go is an attitude. It is also an approach to life. It starts with a desire and a decision to not always make sure that you have all of your bases covered. The ultimate of letting go is in "letting God."

It is the mark of faith to "let God." Part of letting go is the recognition that you are nothing and can do nothing except that which God works through you. Letting go means letting God work through you and, therefore, the power, the gifts, and the glory are all His. Thus, you can be self-accepting while letting the glory be rightly placed fully on God. Letting go through letting God is the way to peace. "But seek first his kingdom and his righteousness, and all these things will be given to you as well. Therefore do not worry about tomorrow, for tomorrow will worry about itself" (Matthew 6:33-34).

In a sense, letting go means to become hopeless. It is a paradox that less hope is sometimes better than more hope. Become hopeless regarding certain beliefs that you have held. Come to terms, for example, with the fact that you will never reach your full potential here on earth. None of us do. Become hopeless about mistake-proofing your life. Know fully that there is no hope in being perfect in action, word, and thought. Realize the hopelessness and futility of earning your salvation through "good" behavior. Letting go means letting God's grace and promises fill your heart. As a result, you are free to relax, back off, and decrease your intensity. You can leave some things undone. You can stop trying so hard.

Letting go is to risk. Risk, by its very nature, entails the relinquishment of control. Healthy risk is best attempted after letting go of the two biggest driving fears, the fear of criticism (the opposite of approval) and the fear of failure (the opposite of achievements). You cannot simply decide to let go of the fear of failure and the fear of criticism. You can, however, decide that criticism and failure are no longer to be avoided at all costs and then live accordingly. Imagine how boldly you would go forth in life if you truly did not worry about being criticized or failing.

The lack of self-acceptance is a great limiter. Part of the price to be paid is the limitation in life choices, options, relationships, new ventures, and pleasures. The fear of letting go forces you into a rigidly controlled, self-protective stance. This is a kind of self-sufficiency that leads to drifting and stagnation. Do you have a sense that you are simply treading water in life or "sitting on the fence"? In what ways do your fears of failure, criticism, and disapproval have you boxed in?

Risking means to try something new. The kinds of risks we are talking about may involve seeking your dreams in the face of appearing foolish. To risk might mean to go after your desires even if they are nonconforming. This might include responding to a calling from God to do something out of the ordinary. Risking is about addressing your needs as if they are important and seeking rest and pleasure even if you then get less work done. Letting go and taking risks can bring about better relationships for you. But these relationships must be sought in the face of the possibility of getting hurt. You will want to try new ventures even if you might fail. You will seek help even if it seems humbling to do so. Other exercises in letting go include expressing yourself and being assertive even at the risk of others not liking you. Risking means that you can be creative even if you might get laughed at. Letting go means to relinquish control even if things might not turn out like you would wish. That is healthy. That is what faith is about.

Keep in mind that not risking is risky in itself. Failure to let go is like being controlled by your need to be in control. If you do not take a chance and try something new, you may look back with regrets. Avoiding the unpleasant often leads to the unpleasant. Nothing is one-hundred percent risk-free. In fact, you unknowingly risk things all the time. Frequently, if you do not know the direction in which to move, it is best to move in some direction, any direction. There are appropriate ways to let go and take risks. We are not talking about headlong, poorly-planned chance-taking, but rather, well-thought-out and reasonable attempts at new behaviors following plenty of prayer. In order to risk wisely, you must let go of the need for certainty. You must let go of seeing yourself as the most important source of strength, wisdom, and salvation. Because risk involves elements of trial and error, it is likely that it will not be all smooth sailing. In fact, plan to mess up, fail, and embarrass yourself. In order to risk, you will face disapproval and new struggles.

You could take some of the fear out of the word "risk" by altering your language somewhat. See the action of "letting go" as "an adventure" or a "challenge." Risking sometimes is simply a trial period in which you "test the waters." How about the phrase, "Send it up a pole and see if it flies?" Have fun, not all risk is serious. See if you can predict the outcome and other peoples' reactions to your new behaviors. Try a new behavior each day. Figure out what letting go would mean to you and try it on for size.

Take a minute to complete each of the following:

> *If I were less afraid of letting go, I*
> *would risk . . .*
> *If I could let go of concern about what*
> *others thought of me, I would*
> *risk . . .*
> *If I were to let go of my fear of failing,*
> *I would risk . . .*
> *If I could let go of my worry about pos-*
> *sible future catastrophes, I would*
> *risk . . .*
> *If I fearlessly pursued my dreams, I*
> *would . . .*
> *If I were to "let go and let God," then I*
> *would . . .*

Self-Worth Without Self-Worship

From the above statements, list out reasonable and potentially beneficial risks that you do not take. Purposefully let go and, with true action and perseverance, actually risk some new behaviors.

Life Experiments
Just like letting go and taking risks involve new behaviors, so does a package of strategies that are called "life experiments." Engaging in life experiments is a good way to turn insight into action. These new behaviors help to solidify any changes that have already occurred in your thinking and feelings. The life experiments listed below encourage you to act as if you are fully self-accepting. In this way, you take on the role of a person who is not struggling with low self-esteem and you live out that role every day until it becomes an integral part of who you are.

Read over the following list and mark the ones that you believe would be a good idea for you to make as part of your own behavioral repertoire. Which behaviors do you need to put into practice in order to help you become more peacefully self-accepting?

1. *Do a self-care activity. Really choose carefully. Put in some effort here and be indulgent. For example, take some time away, treat yourself to something nice, take some extra time for rest, make a new purchase for yourself.*

2. *Do something that is appropriately assertive. Give a gentle "no" to a request, or tell someone that you will no longer accept their abuse and belittlement. Do your assertive behavior prayerfully and without apology.*

3.   *Talk to someone about something that is uncomfortable but potentially fruitful, even if it means exposing yourself or making someone unhappy with you.*

4.   *Do something embarrassing on purpose—spill your water, sing a song in front of others, trip in front of a group.*

5.   *Do something sloppy or half-baked on purpose.*

6.   *Change your mind about something without justifying it to yourself or anyone else.*

7.   *Say "thank you" to a compliment and leave it at that.*

8.   *Release some emotion such as anger (pound some pillows), sadness or grief (allow tears to flow until you are done), joy, or any other feeling that you have had trouble expressing in the past.*

9.   *Talk out loud to yourself. "Wait, am I really a jerk, as I just called myself?" "What is it about my low self-esteem that is making me feel so bothered by that last conversation?" "What are some of the lies that I have lived by and would like to now replace with God's truth?"*

10.   *Allow yourself to be a "little abnormal." Jump around the house in your under-*

wear screaming, "The Martians have landed and I am their king!"

11. *Initiate a new friendship.*

12. *Restart or nurture a relationship or friendship that has faded from lack of contact.*

13. *Get close to someone. Let yourself be in a position to get hurt if things do not work out.*

14. *Trust someone. It is a lie that everyone is out to hurt you.*

15. *If someone criticizes you, ask them for clarification. Ask them what they really meant.*

16. *Do something you have avoided doing simply because you were afraid someone would disapprove.*

17. *Take a stand on a godly position that you believe in, even in the face of challenges, questions, and disagreement from others.*

18. *If you are always with others, practice being alone. Go someplace by yourself. Learn to appreciate times when you are alone with God.*

19. *Let a mess go on around you without cleaning it up. This could be a physical mess or a mess in a relationship.*

20. *Let one of your nonessential relation-ships fade if it has too much anger and misunderstanding in it. Do this espe-cially if trying to fix that relationship has been making you crazy.*

21. *If you find yourself being frequently judgmental of others, let someone's mistake or imperfections go without saying anything about them.*

22. *Make only a so-so impression on pur-pose the next time you meet someone new.*

23. *Try something new that you have avoid-ed out of the fear of being mediocre.*

24. *Ask someone for help.*

25. *Address an injustice and "rock-the-boat."*

26. *Let someone else win, be in the spot-light, take the credit, etc.*

27. *Let someone you know suffer a little if it is the consequence of their own behavior and if your attempts to rescue them have not helped.*

28. *Let someone know of an accomplishment of yours.*

29. *Tell someone something positive about yourself.*

30. *Tell someone about a fear or a silly thought of yours.*

31. *Purposefully build a flaw into something you are doing.*

32. *Find some paperwork that you do not absolutely have to do and throw it away.*

33. *Occasionally take some time to "goof off" and play, even if there is work to be done. Ask the Lord to set healthy boundaries around how much time you work.*

34. *Pray about what other behaviors God might have you try as a life experiment.*

Which of the above ideas sound intriguing or relevant for you? Daily take action in order to gain the most from what you have learned. Do something. Anything. Be creative. Do something crazy. Surprise yourself and someone else.

What you try may not feel like you. Your behaviors may seem a bit phony, artificial, or contrived at first. Push through any early awkwardness and repeat your life experiments until they become comfortable. You may need to work on letting go before trying some of these new behaviors. Do not be controlled by your fears. Do not be controlled by your lack of self-acceptance.

Learning to be Genuine
Perhaps the most salient life experiment involves learning to be yourself around others. Being the *genuine* self as opposed to the *disguised* self can be a

great step forward in the interest of becoming more self-accepting, as well as producing a tremendous amount of relief. It requires, however, a great amount of letting go. Being yourself is the same as stating that Christ's sufficiency is enough. Being yourself is a place of faith where you live out the truth that perfectionism is less important than being perfected. For Paul said in 1 Corinthians 15:10, "But by the grace of God I am what I am, and his grace to me was not without effect . . ." Genuineness means playing the role of the person that God made you to be.

Being genuine is being honest, that is, honest with who you are. It means pleasing God before pleasing man. It means using the gifts that God gave you because you can learn to be less concerned over embarrassment and what others might think. Being real leads to a place of relaxation and peace. Decisions are easier. For example, what opinions you might communicate or what clothes you might wear are based simply on what is in accordance with your own feelings rather than having to decide what would be the most conforming thing to do. Being genuine is the expression of your multidimensionality. This includes being spontaneous, more social, and displaying a fuller expression of every emotion.

Being genuine can cause you to be more firm in your faith, resisting outside pressures and standing up to mockery and even persecution. "Then we will no longer be infants, tossed back and forth by the waves, and blown here and there by every wind of teaching and by the cunning and craftiness of men in their deceitful scheming. Instead, speaking the truth in love, we will in all things grow up into him who is the Head, that is, Christ" (Ephesians 4:14-15).

Self-Worth Without Self-Worship

In what ways are you disingenuous with others? How do you show a disguised self? What kinds of exposure and scrutiny frighten you? You know you are hiding behind the disguised self if:

1. *You never self-disclose.*

2. *You tell someone you agree when you really do not.*

3. *You worry excessively about making a good impression.*

4. *You effortfully cover up any mistakes you make.*

5. *You force an attitude in which you take on an air of nonchalance, confidence, brilliance, etc.*

6. *You act deeply concerned when you are apathetic.*

7. *You never show emotions.*

8. *You never express need or weakness.*

9. *You are overly private.*

10. *You say what you do not mean.*

11. *You figure out what others think before expressing an opinion.*

12. *You choose your words so carefully that your message gets vague and watered down.*

13.   *You lie or exaggerate about yourself.*

14.   *You always wonder how you are coming off in the eyes of others.*

15.   *You always look your absolute best in public.*

16.   *You are a social chameleon. That is, you constantly act like those around you.*

17.   *You are overly compliant and pleasing.*

18.   *You are cool on the outside but anxious on the inside.*

19.   *You feel like a hypocrite and get angry with yourself for going along with the crowd.*

20.   *You hide your talents, gifts, and achievements.*

21.   *You never apologize or admit that you were wrong.*

22.   *You are never able to say, "I do not know."*

23.   *You fail to ask questions out of fear of looking foolish.*

24.   *You stop doing something because no one else is doing it.*

25.   *You invariably tell people you feel "fine" when it sometimes is far from the truth.*

26. *You express yourself indirectly through manipulation, by being passive-aggressive, or by leaving hints.*

27. *You smooth over a problem just to avoid saying how you really feel.*

28. *You quietly accept mistreatment from others.*

29. *You seldom talk.*

30. *You forcefully conjure up enthusiasm and other feelings that are not there.*

31. *You seldom make a decision based on what you would really like.*

32. *You avoid spontaneity in yourself.*

33. *You are aware that you behave in a phony manner around others.*

34. *You are excessively other-oriented.*

35. *You never say or do anything you cannot easily justify to others.*

36. *You apologize when you do not feel at fault.*

37. *You smile or make jokes when you are hurting on the inside.*

38. *You almost always try to meet others' expectations.*

39.   *You express feelings only at the intensity level being shown by those around you.*

40.   *You care more about being "proper" than sincere.*

Do any of the above forty items describe your public behavior? Any time you express, say, or do something that is contrary to how you really feel, you are showing the disguised self. If you feel like you are "selling out" or suppressing your true self, you are not being genuine.

In what ways do you hide behind the uneasy protection of the disguised self? In what circumstances do you say that which you do not really mean? Do you conform too much? Are you both *in* the world and *of* the world more than you would like to admit? Do you over-identify with everyone you are with? What feelings, opinions, and moments of creativity do you withhold? What needs and desires do you deny? How do you avoid exposure and disclosure of self? What is the nature of the roles you play in order to keep others from seeing the real you? What do you know about your own disguised self?

Overuse of the disguised self is exhausting. Being guarded and carefully measuring each word and action takes energy. It is not easy trying to figure out who to be in each different context. Not being genuinely yourself is like saying that your true self is so shameful that it requires being hidden. Living as the disguised self gives victory to the distorted thinking in your life. It is the same as assuming that anyone who really got to know you would most certainly dislike you. Playing life's roles through not being yourself is taking too much control. It is the opposite of letting go, which we now know is a greater place of peace and faith.

It may be helpful to outline some important aspects of yourself and then simply play the role of who you genuinely are. Who are you? What are the deep and enduring features of your character and personality? What are the positions that you hold in life that are most meaningful to you, such as being a parent or an employee? What are your likes and dislikes? What are some of your favorite things? What are some of your pet peeves? What are your most important values and personal principles? What could you say about your spiritual growth and your relationship with the Lord? What motivates you? How emotionally expressive are you? Where do you stand on political issues? What things or persons have impacted your life the most? What are the most important things in your life?

Take time to respond to each question in the above paragraph. "Each one should test his own actions. Then he can take pride in himself, without comparing himself to somebody else" (Galatians 6:4). No one can be you as well as you can. Being genuine is expressing part of God's creation.

There are many lies tied up in your push to be someone you are not. Some of these lies include the ideas that you must prove your worth, never show feelings, see others as superior, be great at what you do, and generally deny the self. Firmly decide now that a fuller disclosure and expression of your true nature is no longer to be avoided. Agree that what God created, even you, is good. Let go and be truer to your identity.

What are some of the advantages of saying what you mean, expressing true feelings, and letting others see the real you? First, it helps you to have a more firm sense of identity because your personality seems more consistent across situations. More open expression of negative feelings, such as sadness, helps these emotions fade more quickly. You will be less accepting of mistreatment. You might be more helpful to others, offering up ideas or even sincere, heartfelt empathy and tenderness without embarrassment. There will be a greater expression of your giftedness and a willingness to be used of God. You will live more in the present and be directed more by internal desires than external pressures. Honesty will prevail as will some originality and healthy risk-taking. Putting on the genuine self will improve your relationships. You will be more spontaneous and fun. Your self-esteem is better when there is congruence among your thoughts, feelings, and actions.

To be genuine means to not mold all your behaviors around what others might do or think. It means "shooting from the hip" with less internal censorship. It means feeling okay about being different. The genuine person expresses all feelings in a timely, though nondestructive manner. Being genuine allows you to address your true needs and preferences. You allow others to see more of the total you, the good and the bad. In social settings you will be less fearful, less shame-filled, and less paranoid. Trying out the genuine self is another life experiment. Watch how others react to you. It could be fun.

As you learn to be more genuine, it is important to remember how much God values you (Matthew 6:26). Even Moses displayed tremendous self-doubt when he said to God, "Who am I, that I should go to Pharaoh to bring the Israelites out of Egypt?" (Exodus 3:11). But God knew that Moses, with all his deficiencies, was enough for Him to use. Moses, an ordinary man who had committed great sin in his life, only needed to make himself, just as he was, available to God. God did not say to Moses, "I want you to be like Abraham." What God did say, in effect, was, "Be willing, be Moses, and trust in Me."

What To Do

1. Go back through this chapter and diligently apply each of the three main strategies: (1) Letting Go, (2) Life Experiments, and (3) Learning to be Genuine. Write out on paper what your goals are and what new behaviors you are going to try.

2. Commit to work on behavioral changes and play these new roles for no less than six months. Live out and make permanent in your actions the important truths that you have learned from this book.

3. Count the costs that you have incurred through stagnation and a fear of trying on new behaviors. Count the costs in your failure to let go and let God. Also count any cost that there may have been in your attempts at being somebody you are not.

4. Keep track of blessings. The blessings here are the benefits that come about as a result of putting your insights into action.

5. Note others' reactions to you as you engage in behavioral changes. As you become more genuine and open with others, see if you can note an increase in other people approaching you and disclosing themselves more fully. Become aware of how your relationships are changing and improving.

6. As you decide which behavioral changes to make, tell someone. Ask a good Christian friend to hold you accountable to your program. Tell the friend that you would like him or her to check in with you occasionally to ask if you are sticking with it.

7. Think of or find Bible verses that support the idea of "letting go." For example, Philippians 4:6 says, "Do not be anxious about anything, but in everything, by prayer and petition, with thanksgiving, present your requests to God."

8. Memorize and meditate on this verse: "I came to you in weakness and fear, and with much trembling. My message and my preaching were not with wise and persuasive words, but with a demonstration of the Spirit's power, so that your faith would not rest on men's wisdom, but on God's power" (St. Paul speaking in 1 Corinthians 2:3-5).

9. Page back through this entire book. Review and refresh your memory for the things that were most meaningful to you. Put into practice what you have learned. Leave this book out where you can see it and be reminded of the new practices which need to continue for some time in order for it to produce any real fruit in your life and in the lives of those around you. And above all this, let the truth of God through Christ work in you. For,

255

"But whoever lives by the truth comes into the light, so that it may be seen plainly that what he has done has been done through God" (John 3:21).

Order Form

Telephone orders: Call 1-800-504-CARE

Postal Orders: Galloway Press
1520 Old Henderson Road, Suite 100
Columbus, Ohio 43220

Please send _____ copies of *Self-Worth Without Self-Worship: The Bible-Based Approach to Self-Acceptance*

Price: $9.95 each, plus shipping $2.25 for the first book $1.25 for each additional (surface shipping may take 3-4 weeks)

Ohio residents add 5.75% sales tax
(Substantial discounts for quantity orders)

Company name: _____

Name: _____

Address: _____

City: _____ State: _____ Zip: _____

THANK YOU FOR YOUR ORDER